Beyond THE PITCH

YOUR GUIDE TO LEVEL UP PUBLIC SPEAKING SKILLS

DR. DIVYA JAITLY

ISBN 979-8-89322-709-3

DEDICATION

My work is dedicated to all those who aspire to become confident, persuasive communicators and leaders.

To the individuals who have a burning desire to make a difference, to inspire change, and to leave a lasting impact through their words, this book is for you. May it serve as a guide, a source of inspiration, and a roadmap to unlocking your full potential as a public speaker and leader.

I dedicate this book to the dreamers, the visionaries, and the believers who refuse to settle for mediocrity. It is your indomitable determination and untiring pursuit of excellence that motivated me. May this book empower you to step onto any stage, virtual or physical, with confidence and conviction, and may your voice resonate with audiences far and wide.

To the aspiring leaders who understand the power of effective communication in shaping strong teams, this book is dedicated to you. May it provide you with the tools, strategies, and insights necessary to communicate your vision, ignite your team, and create a culture of collaboration and growth.

I dedicate this book to the individuals who have faced their fears, embraced vulnerability, and stepped out of their comfort zones in pursuit of personal growth. Your courage and resilience remind me of the transformative power of public speaking. May this book empower you to overcome your fears, embrace your unique voice, and make a profound impact on those around you.

To my Mom and Dad, who have supported me unconditionally throughout this journey, this book is dedicated to you. Your consistent love, encouragement, and belief in me have been my driving force. Thank you for standing by my side, cheering me on, and being my critique and saviour in my down times. Also, I stand refreshed by the indomitable spirit of SHIVYA for adding wings to my dreams.

Finally, I dedicate this book to the readers, the seekers, and the lifelong learners who have chosen to embark on the journey of self-improvement. May this book serve as a source of knowledge, inspiration, and practical guidance as you navigate the path of becoming a more profound communicator and an enigmatic leader.

Dear readers, find the courage to embrace your voice, the confidence to share your message, and the power to create a positive impact in this world.

CONTENTS

Chapter 3: MYTH-BUSTING IN PUBLIC SPEAKING.................. 53

Chapter 4: THE LANGUAGE OF LEADERSHIP 71

Chapter 5: MASTERING NON-VERBAL COMMUNICATION...... 87

Chapter 6: THE SCIENCE OF STORYTELLING........................ 105

Contents

ACKNOWLEDGEMENTS

Writing a book is not a solitary endeavour. It takes the support, guidance, and encouragement of many individuals to bring a project like this to fruition and to arrive at the end of "Beyond The Pitch™ – Your Guide to Level Up Public Speaking Skills; Training Your Voice, Dispelling Myths and Becoming a Better Team Leader". Needless to mention that my deepest gratitude goes to those who have contributed to the creation of this book.

First and foremost, I would like to thank my family for their unwavering support and understanding throughout this journey. Your love, patience, and belief in me have been the foundation upon which I have built this book. Thank you for always being there, cheering me on, and reminding me of the importance of pursuing my passions.

To my friends and colleagues who have provided valuable insights, feedback, and encouragement, I am immensely grateful. Your perspectives and experiences have enriched the content of this book and have helped shape it into what it is today. Thank you for your time, dedication, and willingness to share your expertise.

I would also like to express my appreciation to my team at The Advanced Learning Institute, whose innovative tools and assistance have made the writing process smoother and more efficient. The support has been invaluable and I am thankful for the opportunity to collaborate with such a talented group of experienced individuals.

To my Mentors and Coaches, who have guided me on my journey as a Public Speaker and a conscientious Leader, I extend my deepest sense of obligation. Your wisdom, guidance, and trust in my abilities have been instrumental in my growth and development. Thank you for pushing me to step outside my comfort zone, challenging me to reach new heights, and instilling in me the confidence to share my knowledge with others.

It is truly important to acknowledge the readers and audiences who will embark on their journey of self-improvement through the pages of this book. Your curiosity, willingness to learn, and dedication to personal growth have inspired me and will continue to do so. It is my sincere hope, that the insights and strategies shared in this book will empower you to become more confident, persuasive communicators and 'A Better Version of Yourself.'

Last but not the least, my heartfelt appreciation to all the authors, speakers, and thought leaders, whose work has stimulated and initiated me to pen down these thoughts. The collective wisdom, research, and passion for effective communication have shaped my own understanding and have served as a constant source of motivation.

In closing, I am humbled and honoured to have had the opportunity to write this book. It has been a journey of growth, learning, and self-discovery. Thank you to everyone who has played a part in making this book a reality, I am grateful for your contributions in every step of the way.

Please note: Images used in this book are all AI generated using the generative AI technology.

INTRODUCTION

In the labyrinth of corporate boardrooms, where every spoken word can pivot the trajectory of careers, I stand as a testament to the transformative power of eloquence. With over a decade of cutting through the noise as a freelance consultant, Divya, my name has become synonymous with the alchemy of communication. Whispers of my strategies have echoed from start-up incubators to Fortune 500 roundtables. They speak of a voice that turned trembling speeches into roaring declarations of intent, a voice forged in the crucible of relentless challenge and tireless self-refinement. Have you ever wondered what separates a leader from a speaker? Have you found yourself ensnared by the myths that shroud the art of public speaking in mystery? In the silence that follows a commanding oration, lies the heartbeat of leadership. This is not just a book; it's an odyssey through the spoken word, a blueprint to ascend the peaks of persuasive discourse. And as the curtain rises on this journey, ask yourself—are you ready to command the room?

In the realm of influence, where ideas contend in the arena of public discourse, the mantle of leadership is bestowed on those who command the power of speech. It is here, in the crucible of oratory, that I, Divya, have honed a mastery not often wielded. With each consultation, each workshop, and every keynote, I've distilled not just the essence of commanding communication, but the very ethos of leadership itself.

From the nervous grips of a microphone to the commanding applause of standing ovations, my journey has been nothing short of an odyssey through the spoken word. It's a saga marked by relentless pursuit and profound discovery—a narrative rich with the wisdom of experience. My path has been illuminated by the hard-won insights gleaned from addressing boardrooms brimming with sceptical executives, engaging with diverse audiences across cultural divides, and mentoring emerging leaders to find their voice amidst the cacophony of the corporate world.

The accolades and affirmations of my peers serve not as the end, but as milestones along a continuing journey of growth and contribution. These laurels, while humbling, stand as a testament to the effectiveness of the strategies and techniques I've developed and the lives they've transformed. They are a silent endorsement of the countless hours I've dedicated to this craft—a craft that is both an art and a science.

But what binds us deeper than shared knowledge is the shared struggle—the voice that quivers, the hands that shake, the palpable tension of stepping into the spotlight. My narrative intertwines with the countless individuals who've grappled with the spectre of public speaking, and in that shared vulnerability, an emotional bond is forged. It's in these moments that the true essence of leadership is revealed: the courage to be authentic, the strength to be vulnerable, and the resolve to transform trepidation into triumph.

This book, therefore, is not merely a collection of techniques; it is a prelude to wisdom—a gateway to the empowerment that comes with mastery of the spoken word. The numerous ways I share with you are the keys to unlocking your potential, not just as a speaker, but as a leader who can inspire action, drive change, and articulate a vision with clarity and conviction.

Imagine standing before an audience, feeling the weight of their expectations, the gravity of the moment. Do you falter, or do you flourish?

The answer lies within these pages. As you turn each one, you will embark on a journey that will transcend the conventional and challenge the myths that have held many back from reaching their oratorical potential.

Can you see yourself, as a beacon of confidence, radiating authority as you speak? Envision the barriers falling away as you train your voice to be not just heard, but felt. Picture the transformation from speaking to communicating, from enduring to enjoying, from participating to leading.

This is not just about finding your voice—it's about amplifying it to resonate in the hearts and minds of your listeners. It's about sculpting your narrative, refining your delivery, and elevating your presence. Through these pages, I extend to you an invitation to join an exclusive consortium of enlightenment, where each chapter brings you closer to the zenith of your communicative powers.

So, as we stand on the precipice of this journey, I pose to you a simple yet profound inquiry: Are you ready to transcend the ordinary and embrace the extraordinary power of your voice? Ready to lead, to inspire, to command the room with a newfound poise and purpose?

Let us begin.

CHAPTER 1

THE ART OF PERSUASION

"If you would persuade, you must appeal to interest rather than intellect."

Benjamin Franklin

1.1 Understanding Audience Psychology

In the art of persuasive speaking, the tapestry of words we weave is as crucial as the psychological threads that underpin the listener's experience. Just as a master painter understands the interplay of light and colour, so must a speaker grasp the psychological hues that influence an audience. To unlock the potential of our speech, we delve into the very psyche of those we seek to inspire, to instruct, to move.

As we embark on this exploration of audience psychology, we identify key terms that will serve as our guides through the intricate landscape of the human mind. These terms—attention, emotion, memory, social proof, authority, reciprocity, scarcity, and commitment—will be our beacons, illuminating the path to deeper connection and engagement with our listeners.

Attention, the gatekeeper of perception, determines what experiences enter our conscious mind. Emotion, the vibrant palette of human feeling, colours our thoughts and actions. Memory, the archive of our past, shapes how we interpret and recall information. Social proof, the compass of societal influence, steers our decisions by the actions of others. Authority, the voice of expertise, commands respect and belief. Reciprocity, the dance of give-and-take, fosters goodwill and obliges us in subtle ways. Scarcity, the perception of dwindling resources, heightens our desire for the rare and exclusive. Commitment, the anchor of our identity, compels us to align our actions with our self-image.

Attention is not merely a spotlight; it's a selective beam that can be directed, manipulated, and even hijacked. In a world brimming with distractions, how does one capture and maintain the elusive focus of an audience? Consider the magician who, with a flourish of the hand, commands your gaze—this is the sleight of mind we must achieve through our rhetoric.

Emotion, the heartbeat of our experiences, can elevate a narrative from mundane to memorable. It is the warmth in a voice, the passion behind a cause, the shared laughter or the collective sigh that transforms a speech into an experience.

Memory serves as the canvas where our messages leave an indelible mark. To etch our words into the minds of our audience, we must understand the principles of retention. Like a skilled chef who knows just the right blend of spices, we too must mix repetition, storytelling, and sensory cues to create a memorable feast for the mind.

Social proof, the silent validator, reassures us through the endorsement of others. When we see a standing ovation, hear a chorus of agreement, or read a throng of positive reviews, we are witnessing social proof in action. It is the psychological glue that binds communities and the currency of credibility.

Authority whispers of expertise and experience. In its presence, doubts often yield to nods of agreement. But how does one embody this trait without the traditional trappings of power? Through the confidence in one's voice, the precision of one's words, and the poise of one's stance.

Reciprocity, the subtle art of exchange, can be as simple as the giving of attention to receive it or sharing knowledge to engender trust. It is the unspoken pact that often precedes persuasion, the gentle nudge towards mutual understanding.

Scarcity, the alarm that signals urgency, can be a powerful motivator. When we speak of opportunities as fleeting, of time as precious, of ideas as unique, we tap into a primal instinct to not miss out—to be part of something rare and valuable.

Commitment, the thread that binds our identity to our actions, can be harnessed by inviting small agreements before seeking larger ones. It is the nod before the handshake, the assent before the acclaim, the stepping stones to consensus.

Each of these terms, while individually potent, achieves its true power when interwoven with the others. It's the intricate dance of these psychological elements that captivates an audience and transforms them from passive listeners to active participants.

But how do these abstract terms translate to the tangible world of the speaker? They manifest in the stories we tell, the examples we give, the evidence we present. They live in the contrasts we draw, the questions we pose, the silences we craft. They are the invisible forces that animate our words and the silent partners in every successful speech.

In the world around us, we find rich and relatable examples of these psychological principles in action. The captivating pull of a well-told story, the persuasive power of a respected figure, the influence of friends and neighbours, and the urgency created by limited-time offers—these are the markers of attention, authority, social proof, and scarcity at work in our daily lives.

As we navigate through this journey, we are not seeking a conclusion but a continual unfolding of understanding. There will be no call to action, for the action is implicit in our learning. We do not end with a question because the entire exploration is an inquiry into the soul of audience engagement.

We stand at the threshold of a deeper understanding, poised to delve into the psychological currents that sweep through every gathering of listeners. With this knowledge, we become not just speakers, but architects of experience, crafting moments that resonate, persuade, and ultimately, transform.

1.2 **The Power of Rhetoric**

In the dusky halls of ancient Athens, where the seeds of democracy were first sown, the power of speech was recognized as a force capable of shaping the very foundations of society. It was here, amidst the fervent debates and philosophical discourses, that rhetoric began its ascent to prominence—a tool for the wise and the cunning alike, a means to sway the masses and mould the polis. The ancients understood that words when wielded with mastery, could uplift the spirit, ignite revolutions, or seduce the soul into acquiescence.

As centuries unfurled, the art of rhetoric ebbed and flowed through civilizations, leaving indelible marks upon each epoch. From the pulpit to the parliament, its influence was pervasive. The Renaissance revived classical wisdom, and the Enlightenment shone a light on reason and eloquence. The American Founding Fathers penned speeches that still echo in the annals of history, shaping a nation conceived in liberty and dedicated to the proposition that all men are created equal.

Yet, as the world spun into the age of information, where a deluge of data floods our every waking moment, the ancient art faces a crucible. The modern speaker stands before an audience, not of mere spectators in a forum, but of global citizens interconnected by invisible threads of technology. With this expanse comes a clamour—a cacophony of voices vying for attention, a barrage of images and sounds that dull the senses.

Why, then, does history's lesson in rhetoric hold sway in the digital agora? Because the human heart has not changed in its desire for connection, for stories that resonate, for words that move. We long for the orator who can cut through the noise, who speaks not only with data but with the poetry of conviction, who tells the tales that stir us from apathy.

Imagine the potent silence that envelops a crowd as a leader steps up to the podium, the collective breath held in anticipation. Consider the rapt attention garnered by a speaker who weaves facts with narratives, who knows the pulse of their audience, and speaks directly to it. This is the timeless dance of rhetoric, as relevant now as it was beneath the Mediterranean sun where orators first honed their craft.

At the heart of this book lies the premise that understanding the past arms us with the wisdom to navigate the present. The challenges faced by speakers today are not so different from those of Cicero, Demosthenes, and Chanakya. It is the same quest for persuasion, for imparting knowledge, for inciting action. The medium may have transformed, yet the core remains—the human psyche, with its intricate web of emotions, beliefs, and desires.

Why does this matter now? We live in an era where voices can be amplified to reach the farthest corners of the earth, and where ideas can spread like wildfire. In this vast expanse, understanding how to harness the power of rhetoric is not just valuable; it is imperative. It is the bridge between obscurity and influence, between confusion and clarity.

With each chapter of this book, we will delve deeper into the contemporary exploration of rhetoric's power. We begin by peering into its storied past but soon emerge into the light of today, equipped with the tools to craft messages that resound, inspire, and endure.

Have you ever considered the impact of a well-told story on your own beliefs? Have you felt the pull on your heartstrings, the stirrings of inspiration? This is the realm of the rhetorician—the spellbinding storyteller, the deft debater, the charismatic leader.

Our journey together will be one of discovery, of unlocking the secrets hidden within the folds of history and unfolding them within the context of our modern narrative. The power of rhetoric is not merely a relic of a bygone era; it is the whisper of the past, guiding us through the clamour of today, teaching us how to be heard, how to influence, and how to ignite transformation.

Welcome, then, to the ongoing story of "The Power of Rhetoric." Let us embark on this quest for eloquence, where each page turned is a step towards mastering the art of persuasion in a world that desperately needs voices that can speak not just loudly, but with wisdom and grace.

1.3 Structuring Arguments

Embarking on the quest to master the art of persuasion, we now turn our gaze from the grand tapestry of rhetoric's history to the intimate workings of constructing arguments. This chapter, much like a skilled architect drafting blueprints for a sturdy edifice, will guide you through the meticulous process of building logical and compelling arguments. The goal is clear: to equip you with the ability to craft arguments that not only withstand scrutiny but also captivate attention and sway opinions.

Before you delve into the art of argumentation, it is essential to gather your toolkit. The materials you will need include a solid understanding of logic, a keen awareness of your audience, and a collection of credible evidence. Furthermore, a grasp of the common fallacies that weaken arguments is imperative to avoid pitfalls in your reasoning.

Let us first sketch a broad overview of the steps involved in structuring your argument. Picture a journey, beginning with the establishment of a foundation based on a clear thesis. Next, you erect the pillars of supporting evidence and fortify them with logical reasoning. Finally, you crown your argument with a compelling conclusion that leaves an indelible mark on your audience.

Now, imagine yourself as a sculptor, poised to chisel away at the block of marble before you. Each detailed step in the argumentation process is a deliberate strike that shapes the outcome. Begin by formulating your thesis statement. This is the core of your argument, the claim you intend to prove. It should be concise, specific, and debatable. A well-crafted thesis is like a beacon that guides the rest of your argument.

Next, you must identify the premises that support your thesis. These are the underlying assumptions that form the base of your argument. Ensure that each premise is valid and directly relates to your main claim. Think of these as the load-bearing walls that uphold the structure of your argument.

Once your premises are set, you must gather evidence. This evidence can be in the form of statistics, expert opinions, historical examples, or logical deductions. Each piece of evidence serves as a brick, meticulously placed and cemented with reason. Be vigilant, as even a single faulty brick can compromise the integrity of your argument.

As you present your evidence, be mindful to explain its relevance. It is not enough to simply list data; you must also interpret it, showing how it supports your thesis. Here, the inclusion of vivid imagery can make your argument more memorable: "The statistics on climate change are not just numbers on a page; they are the forewarning of tempests on our horizon, of rising tides that threaten to swallow coastlines and displace millions."

Remember, a strong argument is not merely a collection of facts; it is an orchestra, and you are the conductor. Offer tips and warnings to your reader: avoid overloading with unnecessary details, as this can obscure your main points. Be cautious of fallacies that can weaken your argument, such as 'ad hominem' attacks or false dilemmas.

To verify the success of your argument, test its validity. Invite scrutiny from others, and be open to critique. A robust argument will withstand opposition, much like a fortress endures the onslaught of time and elements.

In the event that your argument encounters rebuttals, do not despair. Troubleshooting is part of the process. When faced with counterarguments, address them head-on. Acknowledge valid points, and revise your argument if necessary. This demonstrates intellectual honesty and strengthens your credibility.

Have you ever witnessed an argument crumble under pressure, its flaws exposed like cracks in a dam? Learn from those moments. Recognize that the power of a well-structured argument lies in its ability to remain afloat even amidst a storm of scepticism.

Incorporate quotations to add authority to your claims. As Aristotle once said, "It is the mark of an educated mind to be able to entertain a thought without accepting it." Encourage your readers to question, to ponder, and to engage with the argument you present.

Now, I ask you, dear reader, to reflect on the arguments you encounter daily. Can you discern the sound structures from the frail? With practice, you will not only recognize them but also create them.

As we journey through the pages of this book, remember that each chapter is a stepping stone towards mastering the subtle art of argumentation. Embrace the rhythm and cadence of persuasive speech, and let your arguments resonate with the clarity of truth and the conviction of belief.

In conclusion, constructing an argument is an art form, a delicate balance between logic and persuasion. It requires diligence, critical thinking, and an unwavering commitment to clarity. With each argument you craft, you are not merely conveying information; you are painting a picture, telling a story, and, ultimately, shaping the world with your words.

1.4 Emotional Resonance

In the vast expanse of communication, it is the profound connection of emotional resonance that truly captivates and engages audiences. As we delve deeper into the labyrinth of effective discourse, we find that the most impactful messages are those that touch the heart as well as the mind. It is here, within this chapter, that we unfold a tapestry of narratives, strategies, and empirical evidence underlining the art of forging such a bond.

Under the umbrella of a bustling cityscape, a local theatre company faced a daunting challenge. This theatre, once the beating heart of the community, had seen waning attendance. The residents, once regular patrons, had turned their attention to the lure of digital entertainment. The theatre's existence teetered on the brink of obscurity.

The main players in this unfolding drama were a passionate director, a dedicated troop of actors, and the community itself, whose collective memory was steeped in the theatre's once-glorious past. The director, a visionary with a deep connection to the stage's power, refused to let this cultural cornerstone crumble.

The core challenge lay in rekindling the community's interest and reviving the theatre's relevance in an age of screens and instant gratification. How could this traditional form of entertainment reclaim its space in the hearts of a distracted populace?

The approach was twofold. First, the company decided to stage productions that mirrored the community's experiences and challenges, thus reflecting their stories on stage. Second, they initiated interactive workshops, inviting locals to partake in the magic of theatre-making. This strategy was not a mere gamble but a calculated endeavour to create a shared experience, a collective heartbeat that resonated with each individual.

The results were palpable. Slowly, the theatre filled with eager spectators, their faces mirroring the emotions played out before them. Attendance numbers soared, and the theatre re-established itself as a hub of community life. The shared experiences led to conversations, which blossomed into a renewed cultural appreciation within the town.

Upon reflection, the success of the theatre's revival could be attributed to the strategic weaving of familiar narratives that echoed the audience's own lives. The interactive nature of the workshops broke down barriers, allowing the audience to step into the world of storytelling and human connection. Although the approach was not without its critics—some deemed it too simplistic—it was the very simplicity that allowed for a universal bond to form.

Visual aids were not necessary in this instance. The power of live performance—its raw energy and immediacy—served as its own visual spectacle, capturing the imagination and stirring the soul.

This case study, rich in its narrative, ties back to the overarching theme of emotional resonance. It serves as a stark reminder that at the core of every message, every story, and every form of art is the undeniable need for an emotional connection. It is this connection that transforms passive observers into active participants.

And now, I leave you with a thought to ponder: In your own endeavours to communicate and connect, how might you weave the thread of emotional resonance through the fabric of your message? How will you ensure that your voice, your story, and your vision resonate with the very essence of those you wish to reach?

The art of emotional resonance is not a mythical narrative of ancient scribes; it is a tangible and powerful tool that, when wielded with care and authenticity, can move mountains. It is the gentle tug at the heartstrings, the momentary glance that speaks volumes, and the shared laughter that echoes through time. As you turn the pages of this book, carry with you the understanding that to truly engage is to feel, and to feel is to be irrevocably changed.

In the end, our messages are but whispers in the wind, yet it is the emotionally charged whispers that linger, that transform, that ultimately define the essence of our shared human experience.

1.5 The Ethos of Credibility

In the vast and intricate web of human interaction, trust forms the bedrock of all meaningful relationships, be it personal or professional. Yet, in an era where information is vast and ubiquitous, the currency of credibility becomes ever more valuable—and ever more elusive. What, then, becomes of the individuals and entities that seek to establish themselves as bastions of knowledge and integrity in their respective spheres? It is this question that we explore in the subsequent chapters, delving into the nuances of credibility, its pivotal role in our society, and the practical means through which it can be cultivated and sustained.

Consider the plight of modern professionals: experts, educators, leaders, and entrepreneurs alike. Each one grapples with the monumental task of not only disseminating knowledge but also ensuring that such knowledge is received with a level of trust that engenders action and change. The problem, stark in its complexity, is a lack of trust bred from a culture of scepticism and misinformation. How does one rise above the dissonance of competing voices to become a beacon of trustworthiness?

The consequences of failing to establish credibility are dire. In the absence of trust, expertise goes unheeded, advice falls on deaf ears, and leadership becomes impotent. Without the confidence of their audience, the professional's influence wanes, and the potential for positive impact is vastly diminished.

So, what is the solution? It begins with the conscious development of an ethos of credibility—a blend of demonstrated expertise, transparent integrity, and the ability to communicate effectively. This trifecta, when cultivated diligently, can elevate one's standing from that of a mere participant in discourse to one of a respected authority.

The implementation of this solution is multifaceted. It requires a steadfast commitment to continuous learning and self-improvement, ensuring that one's knowledge remains both current and comprehensive. It necessitates a personal code of ethics that is unwavering in the face of challenges—integrity must be more than a buzzword; it must be a way of being. And, it demands a mastery of communication—a skill to be honed with the same vigour as any technical expertise.

Evidence of the power of this approach can be seen in the annals of history's great leaders and thinkers, whose legacies are testaments to the enduring nature of credibility. Predicted outcomes suggest that those who adopt this ethos not only engender trust but also inspire others to emulate these principles, thus perpetuating a culture of credibility.

While the path outlined here is robust, alternative solutions merit consideration. Some argue for a more aggressive approach to establishing authority, one that emphasizes bold claims and a dominant presence. Others advocate for leveraging social proof—relying on the endorsements of others to shore up one's credibility.

Yet, what if we gaze beyond the surface, into the heart of the matter? Can you feel the pulse of authenticity that thrives when one's actions align with their words? Does it not speak volumes more than the loudest of proclamations or the most numerous of accolades?

At this juncture, I am reminded of a case that I encountered in the journey of my life —a vignette. A young entrepreneur enters the market with a revolutionary product. Her challenge is not the quality of her offering but the sea of doubt she must navigate to reach her audience. She chooses not a path of boastful advertising or relentless self-promotion. Instead, she offers transparent access to her process, her successes, and her failures. She communicates with candour, providing value through her insights and experiences, and gradually, a community forms around her brand—a community that believes in her because she has proven herself believable.

This scenario underscores the essence of credibility. The entrepreneur's journey exemplifies the power of showing, not telling. Her story unfolds through her actions—a symphony of efforts that resonate with authenticity.

As we venture forth in this exploration, remember that the ethos of credibility is not a mantle easily donned. It is an armour forged in the fires of integrity and expertise, tempered by the hands of effective communication. It is a commitment to oneself and one's audience that, once fulfilled, opens the door to limitless potential.

And so, I pose to you direct questions: How will you weave the fabric of credibility into the tapestry of your professional endeavours? How will you ensure that your legacy is one of trust, respect, and integrity?

Credibility is not a commodity to be bought or sold. It is a treasure to be earned and cherished. As you turn the pages that follow, carry with you the conviction that your pursuit of credibility is not merely a professional endeavour but a personal quest—a quest that, if pursued with purpose and passion, can redefine the very landscape of your influence and impact.

In the end, the ethos of credibility is the silent guardian of your reputation, the unseen ally in your quest for impact, and the quiet whisper that speaks of your legacy long after the clamour has faded. It is the unspoken promise between you and those who choose to listen, a promise that, once made, becomes the bedrock upon which all else is built.

CHAPTER 2

VOICE MASTERY

*"Whilst anyone can use the voice,
few can obtain mastery of it."*

Ajmal Mohammed Bari

2.1 Breath Control Techniques

Unlocking the Power of Your Voice

Imagine standing before an audience, a sea of eyes fixed upon you. Your heart races, but as you draw in a deep, controlled breath, a sense of calm washes over you. With each exhale, your words flow effortlessly, resonating with strength and clarity. This is the power of masterful breath control—a skill that, once honed, can elevate your vocal delivery and stamina to new heights during speeches, performances, and everyday communication.

Before you embark on this transformative journey, ensure you have a quiet space free from distractions. Comfortable attire is key, as it should allow for unrestricted breathing. No special equipment is needed—just your commitment and a willingness to learn.

Envision the path ahead: a series of exercises designed to strengthen your diaphragm, regulate your breathing, and enhance your vocal projection. This broad overview paints the picture of your goal, but let's delve deeper, examining each step with the precision of a craftsman.

Firstly, find your baseline by simply observing your natural breathing. Sit or stand with good posture, and place one hand on your chest and the other on your abdomen. Breathe normally and note which hand rises and falls. The goal is to breathe diaphragmatically, meaning your abdomen should expand, not your chest.

With this awareness, we move to diaphragmatic breathing exercises. Inhale slowly through your nose, feeling your stomach push against your hand. Exhale gently through pursed lips, engaging your abdominal muscles to expel the air. Repeat this process, gradually elongating your breaths each time.

Now, integrate vocalization. On the exhale, produce a sustained "ah" sound, keeping it steady and smooth. This exercise not only reinforces diaphragmatic breathing but also begins to tie the breath to your voice.

As you progress, incorporate speech. Select a text and practice delivering it, paying close attention to where you naturally pause for breath. Mark these spots. Over time, you'll learn to control these pauses, making them work for you rather than against you.

Where might you stumble? Rushed breaths are a common pitfall. Remember, controlled breathing cannot be hurried. Patience is your ally. Also, be mindful of tension in your shoulders or neck, as it can constrict your breathing. Shake out any stiffness before you begin your exercises.

The question then arises, how do we realise that we are on the correct path? Record yourself speaking both before and after practicing these techniques. The difference in your vocal quality and ease of delivery should be both audible and palpable.

Should you encounter persistent difficulties, re-examine your posture and relaxation. Tension is often the culprit in disrupted breath control. If problems persist, consider seeking guidance from a vocal coach.

As you weave these exercises into your daily routine, let the rhythm of your breath become a song, the cadence of a dance. Engage with yourself, asking, "Can you feel the power of your breath as it fills your lungs?" Just pause here and introspect the authenticity of your efforts.

Here I am reminded – "Breathing is the first act of life, and the last," mused renowned opera singer Maria Callas. Her words echo the timeless truth that breath is the foundation of our voice.

In the spirit of showing, not telling, let me share a portrayal. Picture a seasoned orator, poised at the podium. With each breath, the speaker weaves a tapestry of sound that captivates listeners. This could be you.

Through diligent practice, one can transform the very act of breathing into an art form, enhancing not just speeches but enriching life with every breath one takes.

2.2 Vocal Warm-ups and Exercises

From the gentle hum of a seasoned orator to the commanding boom of a theatre performer, the voice can be a powerful instrument. Yet, before it can captivate an audience, it requires tuning, much like a finely crafted violin. The following collection of vocal warm-ups and exercises serves as your personal tuning kit, ensuring that your voice is prepared for the rigors of public speaking.

Imagine the symphony of sounds you could orchestrate with a voice that's both resilient and flexible. The exercises ahead are not simply about making noise; they're a disciplined practice to help you achieve vocal mastery. Consider this your roadmap to vocal excellence, where each step is as crucial as the next.

Let us embark on a journey through the essential vocal warm-ups and exercises designed to elevate the quality and endurance of your voice:

1. Humming
2. Lip Trills
3. Tongue Twisters
4. Resonance Exercises
5. Articulation Drills
6. Breathing for Speech
7. Projection and Power
8. Emotional Expression
9. Cooling Down the Voice

Humming

The simple hum is where we begin, a gentle yet powerful exercise that sets the stage for what's to come. Initiate a soft hum, feeling the vibration across your lips and face. It's like a massage for your vocal cords, promoting blood flow and reducing swelling from overuse or sleep.

Evidence supports the effectiveness of humming. A study published in the Journal of Voice found that humming can increase nitric oxide levels in the sinuses, which is beneficial for respiratory health. This, in turn, can improve voice quality.

Practical applications of a good hum involve starting your day or your speaking session. Humming for a few minutes before a speech helps ease into more robust vocal demands. Transition smoothly into lip trills to further the warm-up process.

Lip Trills

Lip trills, or the lip bubble, require you to blow air through closed lips, creating a brrr-like sound. This exercise promotes relaxation while strengthening the muscles used in speech production.

Vocal coaches often tout the benefits of lip trills for their ability to help singers and speakers modulate their breath control. It's a prime example of how simple actions can have profound effects on vocal performance.

In real-world scenarios, doing lip trills before a presentation ensures that your breath is steady and your voice is less likely to break under the stress of prolonged speaking.

Tongue Twisters

Twist and turn your tongue through complex consonant combinations. "She sells seashells by the seashore" is not just a playful phrase but an exercise that sharpens enunciation.

Renowned speech therapists use tongue twisters as diagnostic tools to identify articulation issues and as exercises to improve diction and speech clarity.

For practical application, practice tongue twisters at varying speeds and volumes to challenge and enhance your articulation muscles. This will prepare you to articulate your words clearly, even in the most nerve-wracking speaking engagements.

Resonance Exercises

Resonance is the richness and depth of your vocal tone. To practice, start with a simple "mee-mah-moo" progression, focusing on feeling the vibration in different areas of your face and chest.

Evidence of resonance's impact comes from actors and singers who rely on resonance to convey emotion and command attention.

Apply these exercises by speaking text with varying degrees of resonance to understand how it affects listener perception and engagement.

Articulation Drills

Articulation drills go beyond tongue twisters, targeting the precision of speech. Repeat a series of plosive sounds p, t, k, b, d. g in which air flow from the lungs is interrupted by closure of mouth. And fricative sounds (f, s, sh) to improve your speech clarity as they are pronounced with the vibrations of the vocal cords.

Speech pathologists have long recommended articulation drills to remedy slurred or unclear speech patterns. Incorporate these drills into your routine to ensure your audience grasps every word during your next public speaking event.

Breathing for Speech

Breathing is not solely about sustaining life; it's the cornerstone of effective speaking. Practice inhaling deeply, then using a controlled exhale to speak. This technique ensures that your words are powered by a steady stream of air.

The practical application of this exercise is monumental. For instance, during a speech, you may need to emphasize a point with great vigour. Proper breath control will allow you to do this without straining your voice.

Projection and Power

Projection is not about yelling; it's about focusing your voice to reach the back of the room without shouting. The "straw technique," where you vocalize through a straw, helps to concentrate your breath and voice, building control.

Theatrical performers often employ projection to reach the farthest corners of an auditorium without microphones. Project your voice during presentations to command attention and convey confidence without coming across as aggressive.

Emotional Expression

Your voice carries emotional weight. Experiment with expressing different emotions through your voice—joy, sadness, excitement, anger. Notice how your tone, pitch, and volume change with each emotion.

Voice actors are a testament to the effectiveness of this exercise, as they often need to convey a wide range of emotions using only their voice. Incorporate emotional expression into your speeches to connect with your audience on a deeper level.

Cooling Down the Voice

Just as athletes cool down after a workout, so should speakers after a speech. Hum softly or do gentle neck stretches to relax the muscles involved in speaking.

A cool-down ritual can prevent vocal fatigue and maintain vocal health, especially after intensive use. Before your next speaking engagement, remember to cool down your voice. This practice can extend the longevity of your vocal health and ensure you're ready for your next performance.

Each warm-up and exercise builds on the next, creating a comprehensive regimen for vocal fitness. They may appear simple, but their impact is profound. As you integrate these practices into your daily routine, remember the power of a well-prepared voice. Your audiences will not only hear but feel the difference.

Will you commit to the discipline required to achieve vocal mastery? The stage awaits!

2.3 Pitch and Tone Variation

Unlocking the Secrets of Engaging Speech

The art of public speaking is akin to a grand performance where every nuance contributes to the overall experience. One such subtlety lies in the mastery of pitch and tone variation—an essential skill that can transform a mundane monologue into a captivating story. This passage delves into the intricacies of using pitch and tone effectively to enchant your audience and communicate with clarity and impact.

When we speak of pitch, we refer to the perceived highness or lowness of a voice, akin to the notes on a musical scale. Tone, on the other hand, conveys emotion and attitude. The interplay between the two can be the difference between engaging your listeners or losing them to the void of disinterest.

Understanding Pitch

Imagine listening to a speech where the speaker's voice remains monotonous, never wavering from a single, flat note. Such a delivery is sure to test the endurance of even the most patient audience. Pitch variation, therefore, is not just a recommendation; it is a necessity for dynamic communication.

To grasp this concept, consider a simple sentence: "The sun set over the horizon." Now, recite it with a rising pitch towards the end, as if expressing awe ! The sentence takes on a new meaning, suggesting a spectacular, almost miraculous sunset. Conversely, pronounce it with a falling pitch, and it might imply the day's end, a conclusion, or a closing chapter. The pitch guides the listener through the landscape of your narrative.

Take the example of Martin Luther King Jr.'s "I Have a Dream" speech. The variations in pitch throughout his delivery turned his words into a melodic and powerful message that still resonates today.

Analyzing Tone

Tone adds colour to the canvas of speech. It's the warmth of empathy, the crackle of excitement, or the icy edge of scorn. It's not just what you say but how you say it that can stir emotions and provoke thought.

Consider the phrase "I can't believe you did that." Spoken with an upbeat, lively tone, it might signal pleasant surprise or admiration. Yet, articulated with a cold, flat tone, it could convey disappointment or disapproval. The tone shapes the context and the message's reception.

Historical speeches are replete with examples where tone made all the difference. Winston Churchill's wartime speeches, laden with a tone of defiant determination, served to inspire a nation under siege.

Incorporating Data and Facts

Studies have shown that speakers who utilize pitch and tone variation are perceived as more persuasive and more confident. A research article in the Journal of Nonverbal Behaviour found that speakers who varied their vocal frequency were rated as more dynamic and attractive. Such evidence underscores the practical benefits of mastering pitch and tone.

Applying Pitch and Tone in Practice

To witness pitch and tone variation in action, observe a seasoned storyteller. They lower their pitch to build suspense, perhaps when a mysterious character enters the tale. They heighten their pitch when conveying surprise or excitement, embodying the characters' emotions as they navigate their adventures.

In your own speaking endeavours, mimic these storytellers. When sharing personal anecdotes, let your voice rise in moments of joy and fall in moments of sorrow, guiding your listeners through the emotional journey. When emphasizing a critical point, adjust your tone to one of seriousness to underscore its importance.

Exploring Different Perspectives

While pitch and tone variation is widely advocated, some cultures may interpret vocal variation differently. In professional settings, for example, too much variation might be seen as lacking seriousness. Hence, it is crucial to consider your audience and the cultural context of your speech.

Clarifying Complex Terms

Pitch and tone should serve to clarify, not confuse. If the topic is complex, a slower pace with clear enunciation can help the audience digest the information. Modulation of pitch and tone can highlight important concepts without overwhelming the listener with vocal acrobatics.

Concluding with Key Takeaways

To encapsulate the essence of pitch and tone variation, remember these key points: variation captivates, tone expresses, and both enrich your speech. They are tools to be wielded with purpose and sensitivity, always tailored to the message and the audience.

As you conclude this chapter and reflect on pitch and tone, ask yourself how you can incorporate these elements into your next speech. Will you rise to the challenge of transforming your delivery from a mere sequence of words to a symphony of meaning? Your voice holds the power to move mountains—use it wisely.

2.4 Articulation and Pronunciation

In the bustling world we inhabit, the ability to communicate with clarity and precision is more than a mere asset; it's a necessity. As the sun peeks through the curtains of a new day, professionals and students alike ready themselves for presentations, interviews, and discussions. Yet, there's a silent adversary many fail to recognize until it's too late—the clarity of their speech.

Imagine standing before an eager audience, your mind brimming with insights. Yet, as you speak, a sea of blank stares meets your gaze. The culprit? Your words, though rich in content, are muddled, and your diction is unclear. Herein lies the crux of our challenge: articulation and pronunciation, the twin guardians of effective communication.

Neglecting the crispness of your speech can lead to misunderstandings, a diminished professional image, and missed opportunities. Like a river that overflows its banks, poor articulation can wash away the impact of even the most eloquent thoughts.

Now, picture a key turning in a lock, opening the door to understanding. Our solution lies in targeted strategies designed to sharpen your enunciation and refine your pronunciation. These methods beckon with the promise of speech that can cut through the noise, ensuring your message not only reaches but resonates with your audience.

To embark on this transformative journey, we must first dissect our language, examining each word as a gem to be polished. Consider the word 'articulation' itself. Slowly pronounce each syllable, and feel your tongue, teeth, and lips form the sounds. This conscious practice is the first step towards impeccable speech.

The implementation of our strategy begins with a daily regimen of vocal exercises. Tongue twisters, for instance, are not mere child's play; they are the calisthenics of speech. "She sells seashells by the seashore," repeated with increasing speed, can fine-tune the instrument of your voice. Additionally, reading aloud from diverse texts—novels, poetry, technical manuals— expands your command over various linguistic terrains.

Evidence of this approach's effectiveness abounds. Consider the transformation of public figures who once stumbled over their words but now speak with enviable clarity. Their secret? A disciplined practice of speech drills and a commitment to continuous improvement.

But let us not don the blinders to alternative paths. Some advocate for technological aids, such as speech recognition software that provides immediate feedback on pronunciation. Others suggest immersion in language through conversation with skilled speakers. While these methods hold merit, they too must be pursued with dedication and a willingness to adapt and grow.

As the sun dips below the horizon, casting a final golden glow, reflect on the power of well-articulated speech. It is the bridge from mind to mind, the vessel for ideas. In the pages that follow, we will delve into the nuances of vocal variety, the subtleties of syllabic emphasis, and the tactics to tackle the thorniest of words.

Consider this: Have you ever truly listened to the cadence of your voice, the symphony of sounds you create? As you do, you'll begin to discover the rhythm in your speech, the ebb and flow that makes conversation musical.

Your voice is your identity.

In the pursuit of simplicity, we eschew the labyrinthine jargon that obfuscates meaning, opting instead for the clarity that empowers understanding. For what is the value of speech if not to be understood?

Throughout our exploration, we'll weave in quotations, the echoes of those who've mastered the art of speech. As the ancient philosopher Aristotle once said, "Speak clearly, if you speak at all; carve every word before you let it fall."

And so, we endeavour not to tell you what to achieve, but to show you the path, lined with anecdotes and illuminated by vivid imagery, leading to a future where your speech is not just heard but felt.

As we close this chapter, remember that articulation and pronunciation are not just about precision; they are about connection. They are the keys to unlocking the full potential of your voice and ensuring that 'The world listens when you speak'.

2.5 Overcoming Speech Impediments

The journey of mastering one's speech is akin to navigating a maze; the path is intricate and demands persistence, but the reward is a treasure of untold value: the power of clear communication. As we delve further into these complexities, we encounter the realm of speech impediments, obstacles that can distort the clarity of our verbal expression. These are not insurmountable walls but hurdles that can be overcome with the right guidance and determination.

For many, the idea of standing before an audience, words flowing with the ease of a gentle stream, remains a distant dream. Speech impediments can act as dams, blocking the flow of communication. But consider this: What if these barriers could be dismantled, brick by brick, word by word?

The claim we examine is bold yet grounded in evidence: Speech impediments, when met with targeted strategies and consistent practice, can be significantly reduced or even overcome. This assertion is not made lightly; it rests upon the concrete foundations of linguistic research and the testimonies of speech therapists and those who have triumphed over their own speech difficulties.

Let's introduce our primary evidence. Studies within the fields of speech pathology and communication disorders suggest that therapeutic interventions, tailored to the individual's specific challenges, can lead to marked improvements in speech. Techniques such as controlled breathing, articulation exercises, and the use of pacing strategies have been shown to be effective in alleviating symptoms of stuttering, lisping, and other common speech impediments.

Delving deeper into this evidence, we unearth success stories that inspire. Take, for example, the case of James, a young man who stuttered so severely that he avoided speaking in public altogether. Through a rigorous regimen of speech therapy, focusing on slow and deliberate articulation, James gradually gained control over his speech. Now, he not only communicates fluently but also enjoys public speaking, a thought that was once unfathomable to him.

However, it would be remiss to overlook counter-evidence. Some argue that certain speech impediments are too deeply ingrained or neurologically based to be completely overcome. They point to studies indicating that neurological development and genetic factors play a role in conditions such as stuttering, suggesting that there may be limits to how much one can improve.

In response, we must clarify that while it's true that some speech impediments have neurological or genetic components, this does not mean improvement is out of reach. The brain's plasticity allows for new neural pathways to be forged with practice. It is not a promise of eradication but rather of progress and enhanced control.

If additional supporting evidence is needed, consider the advancements in technology that aid in speech correction. Devices and applications designed to provide real-time feedback on speech patterns have become valuable tools in the journey toward clearer communication. They serve as modern-day mirrors, reflecting not our physical image but the sound of our voice, allowing for self-correction and reinforcement of proper speech techniques.

As we draw our exploration to a close, let's reinforce our assertion with a final, vivid image. Envision your voice as a finely tuned instrument, each part calibrated to produce a harmonious sound. The process of overcoming speech impediments is like the meticulous tuning of this instrument. It demands attention to detail, patience, and the unwavering belief that each small adjustment contributes to the creation of beautiful music—your clear, confident voice.

Now, pose a direct question: Are you ready to embark on the journey of transforming your speech? With each step taken, and each strategy practiced, the once daunting labyrinth of speech impediments becomes a well-trodden path leading to the heart of effective communication.

Your voice is your identity. It is the vessel that carries your thoughts, ideas, and passions to others. When you speak, the world should not just hear you; it should listen, understand, and be moved. This is the art of communication, and it is within your grasp.

As Aristotle encouraged us to carve our words carefully, let us also remember that it is through perseverance and the courage to face our challenges that we carve our destiny. Overcoming speech impediments is not merely about achieving perfect diction; it is about unlocking the full potential of your voice and embracing the power it holds.

In the chapters to come, we will arm you with the tools and exercises that will guide you through the labyrinth, toward the light of clear communication. Join us on this transformative quest, and let the symphony of your voice resonate with the clarity and confidence that you deserve.

CHAPTER 3

MYTH-BUSTING IN PUBLIC SPEAKING

"99% of the population is afraid of public speaking, and of the remaining 1%, 99% of them have nothing original and interesting to say."

Jarod Kintz

3.1 The Myth of the 'Natural-Born Speaker'

It's a belief as old as oratory itself, etched into the very fabric of public perception: some are born with the gift of gab, the divine spark that sets the 'natural-born speaker' apart from the rest. This assumption, deeply ingrained in our culture, whispers that the art of oration is a privilege of the few, not the skill of the many.

But what happens when this myth is unpacked, dissected, and examined under the unforgiving lens of truth?

The image of the confident, charismatic individual effortlessly captivating an audience is a formidable one. It's a vision that permeates boardrooms, classrooms, and social settings, setting a standard that seems just out of reach for the average person. This ideal creates an invisible barrier, a silent gatekeeper that whispers, "You are not one of them. Don't even try." The impact of this myth is far-reaching, seeding doubt and fear that stifle potential and silence voices.

Consider Swati, a young professional brimming with innovative ideas and a zeal for her industry. Yet, at every team meeting, her voice fades into the background, overshadowed by the louder, more assertive tones of her colleagues. It's not that her ideas lack merit; it's that the myth of the 'natural-born speaker' has convinced her she lacks the inherent talent to be heard. Swati's story is not unique. It echoes in the hearts of countless individuals who have resigned themselves to the audience rather than stepping into the spotlight.

The stakes? They are nothing less than the dreams and ideas that could shape our world. When voices like Swati's are lost, we all suffer the consequences. The next groundbreaking innovation, the solution to a persistent problem, the rallying cry for change—any of these could wither in the shadow of the 'natural-born speaker' myth.

But what if the narrative took an unexpected turn? What if the myth was just that—a fabrication that crumbles upon closer scrutiny? This book dares to tread that path, peeling back layers of misconception to reveal a truth that is both liberating and practical.

The journey ahead is not one of discovering hidden talents but of building them. It's a path paved with determination, strategy, and, most importantly, the understanding that the ability to speak compellingly in public is not a birthright but a skill honed through practice.

Imagine a world where Swati's voice rings out clear and confident, where her ideas are not just heard but embraced. Picture a society unshackled from the myth of the 'natural-born speaker,' where the art of persuasion and the power of public speaking are accessible to all. This is the world this book envisions, a world where the podium is no longer reserved for the chosen few.

Why, then, do we cling to the notion of the 'natural-born speaker'? Perhaps it is because it offers a convenient excuse, a reason to avoid the discomfort of stepping outside our comfort zones. It's easier to believe in innate talent than to face the hard work of self-improvement. But in these pages, you will find not only the inspiration to challenge this myth but also the tools to dismantle it.

Now the crux is, are we set to go on a journey of transformation? Are we prepared to cast aside the fallacy that has held us back? Through a blend of storytelling, empirical evidence, and practical advice, this book will guide step by step, turning the daunting into the achievable.

With each chapter, you'll explore techniques that shatter the illusion of the 'natural-born speaker.' You'll learn how to craft your message, hone your delivery, and captivate your audience. You'll meet individuals who, just like you, once believed that public speaking was beyond their grasp but discovered otherwise through perseverance and practice.

So, ask yourself: are you willing to relinquish the security of the myth? Are you open to the possibility that the power of oratory can be yours? If your pulse quickens with a resounding 'yes,' then let us begin. Together, we'll navigate the misconceptions and emerge with a newfound confidence, ready to take the stage and let your voice be heard.

The myth of the 'natural-born speaker' ends here. Your journey to becoming a remarkable speaker begins now. Welcome to the first step.

3.2 Dispelling Stage Fright

Amidst the bustling throng of a conference hall, where the murmurs of anticipation blend with the shuffling of notes, there stands a podium. It is an unassuming structure of wood and metal, yet it looms like a colossus in the mind of Vijay, a seasoned professional with a wealth of knowledge yet a crippling apprehension of public speaking. His palms are damp, his heart races, and the well-rehearsed words threaten to vanish into the ether of his anxiety. Vijay's struggle is the embodiment of an issue so pervasive that it transcends professions, cultures, and ages: stage fright.

This fear, if left unchecked, can spiral into a self-fulfilling prophecy of failure. The consequences are not merely personal; they are professional. A voice trembles, a mind blanks, and an idea that might have sparked innovation is snuffed out before it can ignite. The cost of this silence reverberates beyond the individual, it stifles collaboration, leadership, and progress.

But what if there was a beacon of hope for those like Vijay, a strategy to navigate the treacherous waters of stage fright? The solution lies not in the elusive quest for innate confidence but in a series of tangible steps that demystify the process of public speaking.

Imagine the transformation if Vijay could channel his nervous energy into a compelling delivery. The first step in this alchemy of anxiety is preparation. A meticulously crafted speech, tailored to the audience and honed to clarity, can be an anchor in the storm of nerves. Preparation extends beyond the words; it encompasses the speaker's familiarity with the venue, the technology, and the nuances of timing.

With the foundation of preparation laid, the next phase is practice. Repeated exposure to the act of speaking, be it in front of a mirror, to a handful of confidants, or even to an empty room, can desensitize the fear response. Practice breeds familiarity, and familiarity is the antithesis of fear.

But what happens when preparation and practice confront the unpredictable reality of a live audience? This is where the art of visualization comes into play. Picturing a successful presentation, feeling the words flow with ease, and envisioning a captivated audience can create a mental blueprint for success. This technique is not mere fanciful thinking; it is a tool employed by athletes and performers alike to prime their minds for victory.

To bolster these internal strategies, one must not overlook the power of physical techniques. Conscious breathing exercises can serve as a tranquilizer to the nervous system, while purposeful movements and gestures can channel nervous energy into a display of confidence.

The evidence for the efficacy of these methods is not merely anecdotal. Studies have shown that individuals who employ a combination of preparation, practice, visualization, and physical techniques experience a significant reduction in stage fright and an improvement in performance.

Yet, there are alternative paths to the same destination. For some, the support of a public speaking group or coach provides a structured environment for growth. Others may find solace in technology, using virtual reality simulations to acclimate to the experience of public speaking. Each of these solutions carries merit, and the most effective approach may be a personalized blend of several strategies.

As the pages of this book unfold, we will delve deeper into each of these solutions. We will explore the intricacies of crafting a message that resonates, the nuances of delivery that captivate, and the techniques that can transform nervous energy into a dynamic force.

Consider now the image of Vijay, standing before the crowd, not as a prisoner of fear, but as a master of his message. His voice is steady, his presence commanding, and his ideas take flight, inspiring change and action. This is the future we envisage, one where stage fright is not an insurmountable barrier but a challenge to be overcome with grace and determination.

So, do you see yourself in Vijay's shoes? Are you ready to confront the spectre of stage fright and claim your place upon the stage of your choosing? If your heart answers with a resolute beat, then join us on this journey. Together, we will dispel the shadows of fear and step into the light of confident expression. The stage awaits.

3.3 The Great Script Debate

In the realm of oratory, where ideas clash and flourish in the crucible of public discourse, two champions emerge: the Script and Extemporaneous Speech. Each holds dominion over its territory, yet its borders are often contested in the great halls of communication. It is in this contested domain that we now find ourselves, seeking to unravel the virtues and vices of each contender.

The significance of our inquiry cannot be overstated, for the choice between scripted precision and extemporaneous authenticity can shape the very essence of a speaker's connection with their audience. The purpose of our exploration is to illuminate the path for speakers such as Vijay, to arm them with the knowledge that will guide their decision in the crucible of public address.

To navigate this debate, we must first establish our criteria. The effectiveness of communication, the adaptability to audience feedback, the authenticity of delivery, and the memorability of the presentation will serve as our benchmarks. With these parameters in place, we can now embark on a balanced examination of the terrain.

Scripted oratory and extemporaneous speaking share the common ground of preparation. Both require a deep understanding of the topic at hand and a clear objective for the speech. A script offers the advantage of precision, each word carefully chosen to convey the desired message, much like a meticulous painting where every stroke is deliberate. Extemporaneous speaking, on the other hand, thrives on the raw spontaneity of thought, akin to an impromptu jazz performance, unpredictable yet enthralling.

Yet, when we shift our gaze to the differences, the contrast is stark. A script is an anchor in the tumultuous sea of public speaking, offering safety and structure. It ensures that no critical point is left unspoken, and no argument unmade. Conversely, extemporaneous speaking is a dance with the unforeseen, a display of the speaker's agility in navigating questions, interruptions, and the subtle cues of their audience.

Imagine a scene where a speaker, armed with nothing but their wits and words, captivates a room. The eyes of the audience follow them, not just listening, but participating in a conversation. This is the power of extemporaneous speech, where the absence of a script cultivates a dynamic and interactive environment.

An analysis of these forms reveals broader implications. A script might lend itself to formal occasions, where precision and formality are paramount. In contrast, extemporaneous speaking might resonate more in settings that value authenticity and connection, such as motivational talks or interactive workshops.

What does this mean in today's fast-paced world, where every word can be amplified through a myriad of digital platforms? The scripted speaker runs the risk of seeming out of touch, their prepared words clashing with the immediacy of social media. The extemporaneous speaker, however, must tread carefully, balancing the need for authenticity with the potential pitfalls of unfiltered expression.

One cannot help but wonder, what if Vijay, the professional plagued by stage fright, could blend these two approaches to create a hybrid that leverages the strengths of both? Could he not harness the security of a script with the vitality of spontaneous speech, thus forging a new paradigm in public speaking?

Let us paint this scenario: Vijay steps onto the stage, his notes at hand, not as a crutch, but as a roadmap. He glances at them, then looks up, connecting with his audience. As he speaks, the words are not recited but lived, his passion palpable in every phrase. The audience leans in, not just hearing, but feeling his message. This is the tapestry we weave when we combine the art of the script with the heart of extemporaneity.

Thus, we arrive at a question that lingers in the air, as tangible as the anticipation before a speech: "Is it better to speak with the certainty of a script or the sincerity of the moment?" The answer to my mind, my fellow seekers of eloquence, is not etched in stone but written in the fluid script of circumstance.

In the end, the choice between a script and extemporaneous speaking is not a binary one. It is a spectrum where each speaker must find their balance, guided by their strengths, their audience, and the message they wish to convey. As we continue to explore the depths of this debate, let us keep in mind that the ultimate goal is not to champion one approach over another, but to empower speakers like Vijay to wield their words with confidence and finesse.

The stage is set, the audience awaits, and the words you choose—be they scripted or sprung from the wellspring of spontaneity—will echo long after the applause fades. So, I ask you, reader, where do you stand in the great script debate?

3.4 **The Power of Silence**

Eight seconds. That's the average length of silence most people can bear before it becomes unbearable, before someone rushes to fill the void with chatter. Yet, in those fleeting moments, a realm of possibility opens—a power so profound that it can transform the ordinary speaker into an unforgettable orator. This is the power of silence.

Why should this fact not just surprise us but also ring deeply with us? In a world saturated with noise, where words often tumble out in torrents, silence can feel like an anomaly. Yet, it is within these quiet interludes that we find the space to think, to breathe, and to connect on a level that transcends the mere exchange of words. The strategic use of pauses and silence is not a void but a bridge, one that leads to deeper understanding and engagement.

As you delve deeper into the fabric of this book, you'll discover that silence is not merely the absence of sound. It is a language in itself, one that can be wielded with precision and intent. The art of mastering this silent tongue is what we will explore together, uncovering its nuances and learning to harness its strength.

Consider this: have you ever been captivated by a speaker who, at the perfect moment, allows his words to fade into a hush, drawing you closer, and making you hang on to his next word? This is no accident, but a careful orchestration of rhythm and expectation. It is in these moments that questions are born and imaginations soar. What is the speaker thinking? What will they say next? How does this silence make you feel?

From the dramatic pause that punctuates a powerful point to the reflective silence that invites introspection, this book will guide you through the myriad ways in which strategic silence can amplify your message. Each chapter will provide you with the insights and techniques to transform silence from an awkward gap into a dynamic tool.

Imagine standing before an audience, your message important, your words carefully chosen. Now, envision yourself weaving silence into your speech, not as an afterthought, but as a key component of your delivery. The impact of your words is no longer confined to their audible expression; it is magnified by the quiet that frames them. This is the journey of discovery that awaits you.

As a freelance consultant, I've witnessed the potency of silence in boardrooms and conference halls across the globe. I've seen it stop people in their tracks, compel them to listen, and drive home points with indelible clarity. Now, I invite you to step into this world of unspoken eloquence, to learn how to use pauses and silence to captivate, persuade, and inspire.

Imagine a canvas—your speech—where the words are the vibrant colours, and the silences are the spaces between. Just as the empty areas give the painting depth, the pauses in your oratory give your words gravity. This book will serve as your palette, offering you the shades of silence to create your masterpiece.

What if I told you that by mastering the art of silence, you could become a more effective communicator than you ever imagined? Would you believe that the spaces between your words could be as compelling as the words themselves? This is not a mere hypothesis, but a reality that has been embraced by the world's greatest speakers and leaders.

It is always important to review the recent conversations you have had! Can you recall a time when a pause, intentional or not, changed the course of the dialogue? Perhaps it allowed you to collect your thoughts, or maybe it gave someone else the opportunity to share theirs. Silence has this transformative power, and this book will teach you to wield it with intention.

As we progress through these pages, you will encounter one-line truths that stand alone in their brevity and impact. These singular sentences will punctuate important concepts, much like how a moment of silence punctuates a speech, inviting you to pause, reflect, and absorb the weight of the words.

In our quest for eloquence, we often overlook the simplest tools. This book strips away the complexity, advocating for simplicity in communication. Through real-life examples, anecdotes, and descriptive language, you'll learn that the most powerful messages are often those that are felt in silence.

You'll hear the whispered wisdom of historical figures and modern influencers alike, each quotation a testament to the enduring power of silence. As you become more attuned to the cadence of speech, you will begin to see how dialogue, both internal and external, is punctuated by the unspoken.

To sum up, this book is not just a collection of strategies; it's a manifesto for those who seek to wield the power of silence. It is a guide for the thoughtful speaker, the reflective leader, and the mindful communicator. Whether you're addressing a crowd, leading a team, or engaging in personal reflection, the principles within these pages will illuminate the path to a more powerful and poignant expression of your ideas.

The journey through will challenge you, inspire you, and ultimately change the way you think about communication. The stage is yours, the silence awaits, and the impact of your newfound eloquence will reflect far beyond the spoken word. So, I ask you, are you ready to embrace the power of the pause?

3.5 Multimedia Misuse

In the realm of public speaking and presentations, the allure of multimedia is undeniable. The promise of vibrant slides, gripping videos, and interactive elements can seduce even the most seasoned presenters into believing that these tools will be the panacea for their audience's engagement. However, as I have observed in my career as a freelance consultant, it is not the tools themselves but how we wield them that determines the success of our communication. This is a narrative of multimedia misuse, a cautionary tale that I hope will illuminate a path to more mindful and impactful use of technology in our presentations.

Picture a large auditorium, buzzing with the anticipation of an expert's keynote speech at a renowned international conference. The air is electric with the collective curiosity of industry professionals, all awaiting insights that could ignite their next big project or idea. This is the scene we set our eyes upon—a moment ripe with potential, a perfect backdrop for our case study on multimedia misuse.

Our main player is Dr. Anshu, a leading figure in cognitive science, known for her groundbreaking research and dynamic speaking style. As she ascends the stage, the audience's applause fades into a hush of expectation. But what follows is a classic example of multimedia misuse that obscures her message rather than amplifying it.

The challenge that Dr. Anshu faces is not uncommon: how to effectively convey complex information in a way that captivates and educates her audience. She begins her presentation with a blitz of slides overloaded with text, intricate graphs, and a kaleidoscope of images that confuse rather than clarify. The core issue here is the dissonance between her spoken content and the visual cacophony that distracts her audience's attention.

In seeking a solution, Dr. Anshu could have embraced the principle of simplicity, adopting a "less is more" approach to her visuals. The most effective strategy would have been to use clean, concise slides that complement her spoken words, not compete with them. By focusing on one key idea per slide and using visuals to reinforce her message, she might have engaged her audience with greater impact.

Regrettably, the results of Dr. Anshu's approach were palpable. The audience, initially leaning in with interest, soon retreated into their devices and whispered side conversations. The disconnect was clear; the misuse of multimedia had diluted the potency of her message rather than strengthened it.

Reflecting on this instance, we can draw broader insights. It's evident that the misuse of visuals can lead to cognitive overload, where the audience struggles to process too much information at once. This can result in disengagement and a failure to communicate effectively. But, by distilling our message and aligning our multimedia use with our objectives, we can avoid such pitfalls.

Visual aids, when applied judiciously, can indeed enhance understanding. For example, a single, well-designed infographic can convey Dr. Anshu's research findings more effectively than ten cluttered slides. Such a graphic, used as a focal point during her presentation, could have served as a powerful catalyst for audience comprehension and retention.

Our story connects to the larger narrative of multimedia misuse in presentations, highlighting the importance of aligning our visual aids with our message. The temptation to use technology for its own sake often leads us astray, away from the essence of our communication. Multimedia should serve as a bridge, not a barrier, between our ideas and our audience.

As we close this chapter, a question lingers: how often have we witnessed or, perhaps, been guilty of overshadowing our message with unnecessary or poorly executed multimedia? This reflection is not an indictment but an invitation to rethink our approach to presentations, to strip away the superfluous, and to champion clarity and purpose in our use of technology.

In your own experiences, have you encountered presentations where the message was lost amid the flash and dazzle of multimedia elements? Can you recall a time when a simple, well-placed visual spoke volumes more than a barrage of slides? These are the moments that challenge us to refine our methods and to embrace the art of simplicity in our visual storytelling.

Our exploration of multimedia misuse is not merely a cautionary tale but a roadmap for those who wish to harness the true power of visuals and technology. As we advance through this book, remember that each tool at our disposal is a double-edged sword. It can either carve a clear path for our message or muddle the trail we wish our audience to follow. Choose wisely, for in the balance hangs the success of our communication and the resonance of our ideas.

In the next chapter, we delve into the psychology behind effective multimedia use, providing you with a deeper understanding of how to captivate your audience's attention and ensure that your message not only lands but sticks. Are you ready to learn how to transform your presentations from forgettable to unforgettable? Let's turn the page and continue our journey into the art of visual eloquence.

CHAPTER 4

THE LANGUAGE OF LEADERSHIP

"A leader is one who knows the way, goes the way, and shows the way."

John Maxwell

4.1 Inspiring Action and Change

Amidst the bustling backdrop of a corporate headquarters pulsing with the steady hum of ambition and enterprise, a quiet tension brewed. At the epicentre of this complex web of glass offices and hushed corridors stood the company's CEO, a figure both revered and scrutinized, grappling with an all-too-familiar spectre: stagnation.

The CEO, known for her incisive intellect and steely resolve, had weathered many a storm. Yet, as the market evolved at a breakneck speed, her once-dominant firm found itself at a crossroads, struggling to keep pace with the relentless march of innovation. Her name was Apoorva, and she was about to embark on a journey that would not only redefine her leadership but also serve as a beacon for those who sought to enact change through the power of oration.

The challenge laid bare before Apoorva was multifaceted: a workforce mired in complacency, competitors who deftly maneuvered to usurp her company's foothold, and an industry that seemed to mutate with each passing quarter. The urgency for transformation was palpable, yet the path forward remained shrouded in uncertainty.

Undeterred, Apoorva resolved to galvanize her organization through a series of meticulously crafted speeches, designed to ignite a collective drive and propel the company toward a renaissance of innovation and growth. Her strategy hinged on the ancient art of rhetoric, yet was infused with modern insights into organizational psychology and motivational dynamics.

She commenced her crusade in the company auditorium, a cavernous space now teeming with expectant faces. Her voice, clear and resonant, cut through the murmurs, "We stand on the precipice of a new era," she began, her cadence measured, her gaze unwavering. "An era that demands not just our attention, but our unwavering commitment to adapt, innovate, and lead."

Apoorva's approach was methodical. She crafted narratives that spoke to both the heart and the intellect, weaving statistics with storied examples of past triumphs. Her speeches were punctuated with rhetorical questions that probed the minds of her audience, "What legacy shall we leave? Will we be the architects of our future or its bystanders?"

The results were not immediate, but they were profound. Over the following months, a transformation swept through the organization. Productivity surged, novel ideas emerged, and morale soared. The data spoke volumes: employee engagement scores climbed by 30%, while market share saw a significant uptick.

In her reflection, Apoorva analyzed the efficacy of her approach, acknowledging that while her words were the spark, the true change came from the belief instilled in her team. She pondered the nuances of her message delivery, considering whether a less direct approach might have fostered an even deeper sense of ownership among her staff.

To illustrate her journey, she incorporated visual aids in subsequent presentations—graphs showing performance metrics, photographs capturing moments of team collaboration, and diagrams outlining the roadmap for the future. These images served not only as evidence of progress but also as a shared vision that everyone could rally behind.

This case study, a microcosm of leadership in action, reverberated with broader implications for inspiring change. It underscored the notion that the words of a leader when wielded with precision and passion, could become the catalyst for collective transformation.

This all leads to a lingering thought hanging in the air, a question for the reader to ponder: "If the words we speak have the power to move mountains, what mountains will you choose to move?"

The echo of that question rippled through the corridors of the mind, inviting leaders, visionaries, and dreamers alike to consider their potential for inspiring action and change.

4.2 Communicating Vision

In the wake of Apoorva's tale, where the spoken word became the fulcrum of organizational change, lies a broader truth: the ability to communicate a vision is not merely the purview of CEOs and industry titans. It is an art that can be mastered by anyone who aspires to lead, to influence, or to inspire. Whether you're a budding entrepreneur, a community leader, or a head of a small team, the power to articulate a vision that captivates and mobilizes people is a transformative skill.

The goal for you, the reader, is clear: to develop the prowess to convey your vision in such a way that it resonates deeply with your audience, compelling them to join you on a journey toward a shared destination. To achieve this, you must first lay the groundwork with several prerequisites. You will need a deep understanding of your vision, a thorough knowledge of your audience, and a mastery of the techniques that will be outlined herein.

As you embark on this journey, visualize a roadmap spread out before you, each stop representing a crucial phase in the process of communicating your vision. The overview of this path is straightforward: establish your vision, know your audience, craft your message, deliver with impact, engage through interaction, and finally, ensure your vision takes hold.

Let's explore the detailed steps of this process. Begin by defining your vision with utmost clarity. It must be vivid, tangible, and imbued with a sense of purpose that transcends the mundane. Next, step into the shoes of those you wish to influence. Understand their aspirations, fears, and the unspoken narratives that shape their worldview.

With this foundation, sculpt your message. Construct a narrative that is both logical and emotive, a tapestry interwoven with facts and stories that illustrate the brighter future you envision. As you do so, remember to speak not just to the mind but also to the heart.

When it comes time to deliver your vision, do so with conviction. Use a voice that is firm yet inviting, gestures that reinforce your words, and an authenticity that fosters trust. Paint your vision not with drab data alone but with the rich colours of anecdotes and experiences that bring it to life. Engage your audience by posing questions that stir reflection. "Imagine what we could achieve if...?" Allow the audience to contemplate and relate with a personal connection with your vision.

As you weave through these steps, heed this advice: be concise, for brevity often breeds clarity. Caution against overpromising; the gap between grandiose words and reality can swiftly erode trust. And maintain a flexible stance, for a vision that cannot adapt to unforeseen circumstances is like a tree that snaps in a strong wind.

To validate that your vision has been effectively communicated, look for signs of engagement: nods of agreement, sparked conversations, and, most tellingly, the initiation of action. When your audience begins to echo your vision in their language and deeds, you'll know it has taken root.

However, be prepared for challenges. You may encounter scepticism or inertia. When faced with such hurdles, listen earnestly, address concerns with evidence and empathy, and, if necessary, refine your vision without diluting its essence.

Throughout this exploration, the following points have been emphasized: clarity of vision, understanding of audience, narrative crafting, impactful delivery, interactive engagement, and ensuring the vision's adoption. Each is a brushstroke in the larger picture of effective communication.

Consider what vision lies within you yearning for expression and then convert it into thoughts and ideas, not only to inform but to transform. Let the journey continue.

4.3 The Art of Feedback

In the buzzing hum of the modern workplace, where ideas spark and ambitions soar, lies a potent yet often underutilized tool: feedback. It's the lifeblood of professional growth, the catalyst for performance enhancement. Yet, feedback is frequently mishandled, its delivery fraught with discomfort, and its reception met with defensiveness. It begs the question: How can we harness the true power of feedback to uplift rather than deflate?

Navigating the treacherous waters of communication, we encounter our primary challenge: to provide constructive feedback that is both heard and heeded. When delivered with care, feedback can illuminate the path to excellence, but when mishandled, it can extinguish the very spark that drives progress.

Imagine the impact on a team where feedback is shunned due to fear of conflict or misinterpreted as personal criticism. The consequences are manifold: stifled innovation, eroded morale, and a breeding ground for mistakes that go uncorrected. It's like walking through a minefield blindfolded, each step a potential misstep with far-reaching repercussions.

But what if we could transform this dynamic? What if feedback became a bridge to understanding, a dialogue that fosters improvement and fortifies relationships? The solution lies in mastering the art of delivering feedback with a careful blend of honesty and empathy.

To embark on this transformative journey, begin by setting the stage for a constructive exchange. This requires an environment of trust where feedback is not an ambush but an expected and integral part of the workflow. It's about crafting a culture where feedback is perceived as a gift, not a weapon.

The next step is to learn the nuances of effective feedback delivery. It starts with the acknowledgment that feedback is not about asserting authority but about guiding growth. It is a dialogue, not a monologue, a shared exploration of how to excel together. Begin your feedback with affirmations of the individual's strengths, then proceed to areas that need improvement. Be specific, focus on behaviour rather than personality, and provide actionable suggestions. For example, rather than pointing out somebodies lack of involvement, try nudging them to share their insightful ideas for greater interactions.

But how do you ensure that your feedback is not just delivered but also embraced and acted upon? The implementation stage is crucial. It requires follow-up, resources, and sometimes, training to help the recipient translate feedback into action. It's akin to giving someone the destination for a treasure hunt but also providing the map and tools necessary to reach it.

Evidence of the effectiveness of this approach abounds. Consider a study by Gallup which revealed that employees who receive regular feedback are three times more likely to be engaged at work than those who do not. Engagement, in turn, is linked to higher productivity, better retention rates, and more innovation.

While this approach is powerful, alternative methods may also yield positive results. Some advocate for the "sandwich method," where critical feedback is nestled between two positive statements. However, this strategy can sometimes obscure the message or make praise seem insincere. It's important to evaluate the context and the individual when deciding on the best approach.

In summary, the art of feedback is a delicate dance that, when performed correctly, can elevate an entire organization. It's about fostering an environment where feedback is expected and welcomed, delivering it with precision and empathy, and supporting its implementation with actionable steps. It's about shifting the perspective from feedback as criticism to feedback as a cornerstone of continuous improvement.

As you turn the page, reflect on this: How often do you give and receive feedback in a way that truly contributes to growth? The art of feedback is not just in its delivery but also in its acceptance and utilization. May this chapter serve as a guide to mastering this invaluable skill, propelling you and those around you to heights unimagined. Let the conversation begin.

4.4 Leading Through Storytelling

In the dappled light of an early morning, a seasoned CEO stood before a hushed assembly of eager-eyed employees, the air thick with anticipation. This was a man known for his commanding presence, yet today, he seemed different—vulnerable, even. He cleared his throat, glanced around the room, and began to speak, not of targets and strategies, but of a time when he, too, stood on uncertain ground, grappling with choices that would define his career.

His story was not one of numbers and charts but of people and paths crossed, of a mentor who had once taken him aside after a particularly disheartening board meeting. The mentor's words were simple yet profound, "The charts will fade, the numbers will be forgotten, but the stories we shape and the lives we touch will outlast our tenure." That wisdom had anchored him through storms of doubt, steering his leadership toward a legacy of human connections.

With each word, the CEO wove a narrative tapestry, rich with the threads of his triumphs and tribulations. The employees leaned in, seeing in his journey a mirror of their aspirations and fears—the universal quest for meaning in the labyrinth of corporate life. The unexpected vulnerability of their leader bridged the gap between hierarchies, and in that moment, a new chapter of company culture was penned.

As the silence settled like dust after his tale, the CEO looked around at the faces before him. "What stories do you carry?" He enquired, inviting a shared saga of discovery regarding the lessons that have had a formative influence in their life's journey."

This, dear reader, is the essence of Leading Through Storytelling. I am Divya, a freelance consultant with a penchant for unravelling the human elements that drive organizational success. In these pages, you will uncover the power of narrative to not only captivate but to catalyse change, to transform leadership from a role into a resonant journey that others are compelled to follow.

The importance of storytelling in leadership is not a new revelation, but its practice remains elusive to many. Stories are the vessels of our values, the currency of our experiences, and the blueprint for our collective aspirations. They resonate on a frequency that facts alone cannot reach, striking chords of empathy and understanding that bind leaders to listeners.

Consider the parables of old or the biographies of world-changers; they endure not for the dates or data they contain but for the struggles they depict, and the human spirit they celebrate. Your leadership narrative has the same potential to endure, to ignite a fire in the hearts of those you lead. But how do you craft such stories, and more importantly, how do you wield them with intention?

The journey of Leading Through Storytelling is not a linear path but a spiral, ever-deepening into the core of what makes us human. As we delve into the craft, we will explore the elements of a compelling story—character, conflict, resolution—and how they parallel the challenges and triumphs of leadership. We will dissect the anatomy of narratives that have shaped history and extract the marrow of their message to fortify our storytelling skills.

Along the way, I invite you to pause and reflect: What is the narrative that you have been a part of? What tales of resilience, innovation, or transformation can you share to illustrate the values you stand for? How can you harness these stories to not only inform but to transform those around you?

In the pages to come, we will also confront the pitfalls of storytelling in leadership—the temptation to embellish, to dominate the narrative, or to lose authenticity amidst the crafting. We will learn to navigate these hazards with grace, ensuring our stories remain beacons of truth and trust.

Storytelling is not a tool of deception but a medium of deep connection. It is the art of painting visions that others can see themselves in, of crafting echoes that resonate with the timbre of our shared humanity.

As you immerse yourself in the following chapters, I offer you not just insights but an invitation: to become not just a leader, but a storyteller, a weaver of dreams, and a guide through the wilderness of the corporate world. Your audience awaits, and your stories beckon. Let us begin the journey together.

4.5 Crisis Communication

In the aftermath of upheaval, where do we turn? A crisis looms, and the organization stands at the precipice of uncertainty. The ground quakes beneath the foundations of meticulously laid plans, and the air crackles with the tension of impending decisions. At this critical juncture, the power of communication becomes the beacon that guides the ship through stormy waters.

When chaos unfurls its wings, organizations face a formidable adversary, misinformation. It spreads like wildfire, unchecked, breeding panic and discord. The primary challenge, then, is clear—how to quell the flames of confusion with the soothing balm of clarity?

Left unaddressed, the consequences of a communication vacuum are dire: trust erodes, reputations crumble, and the bond between brand and stakeholder frays. A tarnished image might haunt an organization long after the crisis has passed, like a shadow clinging to its history.

But what if there was a way to navigate through the maelstrom with poise? Imagine a strategy not only reactive but proactive, one that turns the tide of crisis into an opportunity for growth and fortitude.

The solution lies in a robust crisis communication plan, a blueprint for dialogue in the eye of the storm. Constructing this plan demands a keen understanding of the landscape and a map of the terrain where the crisis unfolds. It requires an intimate knowledge of the stakeholders involved, their concerns, and how best to address them.

To implement this strategy, one must first establish a crisis communication team, a group of individuals adept at the art of messaging and swift in their response. This team becomes the voice of the organization, steering the narrative with precision and care.

Within the tumult, communication must be clear, consistent, and transparent. This trinity forms the cornerstone of trust, a trust that once broken, is a Herculean task to restore. Each message delivered should be crafted with the intent to inform, to reassure, and to guide.

But how do we know if the strategy works? Evidence comes from the calm that follows the storm, the return to equilibrium. Organizations that have weathered crises and emerged stronger share a common thread—a commitment to open, honest, and timely communication.

What about alternative solutions? Some propose silence, a lockdown of information as a protective shell. Yet, history has shown that silence often breeds speculation, and speculation is a beast of its own making. Others suggest a defensive stance, a refutation of all claims. However, this approach risks alienating those seeking solace and answers.

In the labyrinth of crisis management, communication is the thread guiding us out of the darkness. It is the strategy that transforms victims into victors, the language that speaks of resilience rather than defeat.

Consider the case of a well-known airline that faced the unthinkable—a tragedy in the skies. Their response? Immediate acknowledgment of the incident, a promise to prioritize the needs of affected families, and a commitment to transparency throughout the investigation. The airline's forthright approach garnered respect and paved the way for recovery.

In your organization, when faced with adversity, will you allow rumour to dictate the narrative? Or will you seize the reins of communication, crafting messages that resonate with truth and empathy?

This is not just a call to action but a call to arms. The battle may be against forces unseen, but the weapons we wield are words and the manner in which we deploy them. To master crisis communication is to understand the human heart—the fears that drive us, the hopes that sustain us.

As you turn the page, remember that the strategies herein are not static. They are as dynamic as the crises they aim to address. They require adaptation, evolution, and above all, an unwavering commitment to the truth.

The journey through these chapters will arm you with more than tactics; it will furnish you with the insight to discern the nuances of crisis communication, and to apply its principles with discernment and tact.

The story of your organization is being written each day. In times of crisis, will it be a tale of triumph or a lesson in what could have been? The pen is in your hands, the script yet unfinished. Let the dialogue begin.

CHAPTER 5

MASTERING NON-VERBAL COMMUNICATION

"The most important thing in communication is hearing what isn't said."

Peter F Drucker

5.1 The Power of Posture

In an amphitheatre thronged with eager faces, a lone figure strides to the centre stage. The crowd hushes as the individual stands tall, shoulders squared and head held high in a confident manner. Without uttering a single word, the audience is captivated, drawn to the commanding presence before them. This silent introduction speaks volumes, demonstrating the profound impact of posture on perception and influence.

What is it about posture that can so dramatically affect the way we are perceived by others? And more importantly, how can it be harnessed to exude confidence and command attention? Let's delve into the world of nonverbal communication to uncover the power that lies within the way we carry ourselves.

At the heart of this exploration is the assertion that posture is a key determinant of how individuals are judged in terms of authority, confidence, and professionalism. An upright stance is often associated with a sense of self-assurance and dominance, while a slouched form can convey uncertainty or submissiveness.

To substantiate this claim, a plethora of studies have been conducted, one of which is a ground breaking research project led by social psychologist Amy Cuddy. Her work revealed that adopting a "power pose" – standing in a posture of confidence, even when we do not feel confident – can affect testosterone and cortisol levels affecting our chances of success by boosting the state of our mind.

By examining this evidence, it becomes apparent how posture can affect not only how others perceive us but also how we perceive ourselves. Cuddy's research suggests that the act of standing tall can foster an internal psychological state that bolsters a person's courage and ability to handle stressful situations.

However, it would be negligent to disregard the voices that caution against an oversimplified view of posture's influence. Critics argue that the effects of posture on psychological states are not as strong or reliable as some researchers propose. They contend that individual responses to posture manipulation can vary significantly and that the context in which a person is placed plays a crucial role.

In response to these counterarguments, it is essential to clarify that while posture is not a panacea for insecurity or a guaranteed method for achieving success, it is one component of a multifaceted approach to enhancing personal presence and influence. It acts in concert with other factors such as tone of voice, eye contact, and attire to create an overall impression.

Further supporting evidence can be found in the world of theatre and performance, where actors are trained rigorously in the use of body language to convey complex emotions and characters. The precise control and conscious manipulation of posture enable them to project an aura of confidence or vulnerability as required by their roles.

In conclusion, the claim that posture has the power to convey confidence and command attention is reinforced through both scientific research and practical examples. A poised stance can serve as a nonverbal cue that sets the stage for positive engagement, reflecting an inner state of readiness and control. As we navigate the theatres of our professional and personal lives, let us be mindful of the silent but potent language of our bodies. In the end, the way we carry ourselves can shape not only how we are seen, but also who we become.

5.2 Facial Expressions and Eye Contact

Facial expressions and eye contact are the silent orchestrators of human connection. As we delve into this critical aspect of nonverbal communication, we unveil the subtle yet profound ways in which our faces and eyes can articulate a narrative, influence emotions, and build relationships without uttering a single word.

A smile, a frown, a look of surprise – our faces can express a gamut of emotions, each sending a distinct message to the observer. When we engage with others, our facial expressions act as a mirror reflecting our internal states, often bypassing the need for verbal articulation. The creases of a smile can signal warmth and approachability, inviting others into our space. Conversely, a furrowed brow might indicate concern or contemplation, prompting an observer to offer support or maintain a respectful distance.

But what is it about these expressions that carry such weight in communication? The human brain is hardwired to recognize and interpret facial cues. This ability to read faces is essential for survival, allowing us to quickly assess intentions and respond accordingly. In social interactions, this means our expressions can either foster connections or create barriers. Studies have shown that individuals who employ a diverse range of facial expressions are often perceived as more empathetic and socially adept.

Consider, for instance, the way a leader might use expressions to inspire their team. A look of determination can galvanize a group, while a genuine smile in times of success can reinforce a sense of camaraderie. In contrast, imagine the chilling effect of an impassive, unreadable face during a critical discussion – the lack of expression can sow seeds of doubt and unease.

Eye contact, the twin force to facial expressions, is equally potent. It's often said that the eyes are the windows to the soul, revealing truths that words might strive to conceal. Maintaining eye contact during a conversation signals interest and respect, forging a bond that fosters trust and understanding. When we look into someone's eyes, we are seeking a glimpse of authenticity, a confirmation that we are truly being seen and heard.

The power of eye contact has been substantiated by numerous psychological studies. When individuals lock gazes, even for brief moments, they can synchronize their brainwaves, leading to increased empathy and mutual understanding. Yet, the nuances of eye contact vary across cultures and contexts. What is considered attentive and respectful in one culture might be seen as challenging or disrespectful in another. It's this delicate balance that we must navigate to effectively utilize eye contact in our interactions.

Still, have you ever considered how too much eye contact can be as disconcerting as too little? The art lies in moderation. For example, a speaker who never breaks eye contact might come across as intimidating, while one who frequently averts their gaze could appear disinterested or untrustworthy.

Striking the right balance requires a dance between speaker and listener – a responsive ebb and flow of looking and looking away that respects personal boundaries while still maintaining connection.

Let us take a moment to ponder: How often do we consciously adjust our facial expressions or eye contact to influence a situation? Are we aware of the signals we send with just a glance or a subtle change in expression?

It's critical to recognize that not all complex emotions or thoughts can be translated into words with the same ease or clarity. At times, our faces do the talking for us. A compassionate tilt of the head, a quizzical raise of an eyebrow, or the unwavering attention of our gaze can communicate volumes, transcending the barriers of language.

In conclusion, the intricate dance of facial expressions and eye contact is a testament to the nuanced art of human interaction. As we navigate the complexities of communication, let us remember that our faces and eyes can be powerful tools in conveying sincerity, fostering relationships, and ultimately, connecting with the world around us. The messages we send through these silent cues can enhance our narratives, making every glance and every expression a pivotal verse in the story of our interwoven lives.

5.3 Gestures That Enhance Your Message

The art of communication extends far beyond the spoken word; it is the harmonious blend of voice, expression, and physicality that truly conveys a message. Where words may falter, gestures step in, accentuating and underscoring our intentions with silent but emphatic strokes. As we explore the rich tapestry of body language, we discover the gestures that not only complement our words but elevate them, infusing them with a potency that resonates with our audience.

In the theatre of everyday conversation, our hands are the conductors orchestrating the rhythm and emphasis of our dialogue. They can build bridges of understanding or raise walls of confusion. It is with this in mind that we delve into the gestures that, when used judiciously, have the power to transform the mundane into the memorable.

Gesture: the Palm-Up Position

Unveiling Trust and Openness

The palm-up gesture is a universal sign of honesty and submission. In the same way that an open hand can signal a lack of weapons in ancient times, exposing one's palms during conversation suggests that one has nothing to hide. This simple movement can create an atmosphere of trust and invite collaboration.

Supporting the Claim

Research in the field of nonverbal communication has shown that speakers who use open-palm gestures are often perceived as more agreeable and persuasive. The findings suggest that this gesture taps into deeply rooted responses, engendering a sense of safety and acceptance in the observer.

Bringing Theory to Life

Imagine a leader addressing their team about an upcoming challenge. With palms facing up, they express their concerns and invite input. This non-threatening stance encourages team members to speak openly, fostering a culture of shared responsibility and innovation. The palm-up gesture thus becomes a catalyst for collective problem-solving and unity.

Gesture: The Precision Grip

Conveying Detail and Accuracy

The precision grip—where the thumb and fingers come together as if holding an invisible object—suggests exactitude and attention to detail. It is the physical manifestation of pinpointing a fact or honing in on specifics. When a speaker employs this gesture, they draw their audience's attention to the fine print, to the nuances that merit scrutiny.

Evidence of Effectiveness

Studies in gesture efficacy indicate that the precision grip can enhance the perceived intelligence and meticulousness of the speaker. It is a visual cue that aligns with verbal messages of specificity, reinforcing the speaker's command over the subject matter.

Practical Applications

Consider a scientist explaining a complex concept. As they reach the crux of their explanation, their fingers come together in a precision grip. This subtle cue signals to the listeners that what follows is crucial and warrants their undivided attention. The message is not just heard—it is seen and understood at a deeper level.

Gesture: The Steeple

Projecting Confidence and Authority

The steeple, where fingertips touch to form a peak, is often associated with confidence and self-assuredness. It is a gesture that conveys authority without aggression, a quiet assertion of one's expertise or status. When used appropriately, it can lend weight to a speaker's words, projecting an aura of control and mastery.

Anecdotal and Empirical Support

Anecdotes from seasoned public speakers, as well as experimental studies, suggest that the steeple gesture can positively influence an audience's perception of the speaker's credibility. It is a nonverbal endorsement of one's assertions, one that can sway listeners towards agreement and acceptance.

Application in Action

A CEO delivering a strategic vision might interlace his fingers in a steeple as they emphasize key points. This gesture, coupled with a steady gaze and measured tone, radiates confidence, assuring stakeholders of the soundness of the proposed direction. The steeple becomes an unspoken guarantee of the speaker's belief in their message.

Gesture: The Chop

Emphasizing Points and Signalling Determination

The chopping motion—where the edge of the hand cuts through the air—can be a powerful tool for underlining important points or displaying resolve. It is a bold gesture that breaks through the noise, commanding attention and underscoring the significance of certain statements.

Backing Up the Chop

Research has shown that the chop is particularly effective in scenarios that call for clear, decisive communication. It cuts to the heart of the matter, visually partitioning the essential from the extraneous.

Real-World Relevance

In a debate, a politician might use the chop to drive home a core argument. Each precise motion aligns with a key point, visually punctuating their commitment to the issue. The audience is left with no doubt about the speaker's stance—each chop, a mark of their resolve.

As we thread our way through the language of gestures, we must be mindful of the delicate interplay between motion and meaning. The dance of hands in space is not merely an accompaniment to words; it is a language unto itself, capable of conveying subtleties and inspiring convictions. Let us harness this language with intention and grace, allowing our gestures to speak volumes in the silence between words.

5.4 Dress for Success

In an age where communication is often relegated to the swiftness of a text message or the brevity of a tweet, the power of in-person interactions has become increasingly significant. It is within this realm that attire and personal grooming speak volumes before a word is even uttered. The adage "dress for success" is not merely a throwaway phrase—it is psychological armour and a strategic tool in the art of persuasion and influence.

Imagine stepping onto a stage. The spotlight hits, the audience hushes, and all eyes turn towards you. Before the dialogue begins, your appearance has already commenced a silent conversation. What does it say? Does it speak of professionalism, competence, and credibility, or does it murmur of neglect and indifference?

The crux of the matter lies in the nonverbal cues that attire and grooming emit. They are the unspoken heralds of your personal brand, potentially casting shadows of doubt or rays of confidence in the minds of your audience. When misaligned with the intended message, these visual signals can create dissonance, diluting the potency of your words and leading to a diminished impact on your overall presentation.

The consequences of such oversight can be dire. In the professional sphere, a speaker's appearance that is not congruent with their message can lead to lost opportunities, diminished authority, and a weakened ability to lead or influence. The business world is rife with tales of pitches gone awry and negotiations soured, all stemming from a disconnect between the speaker's appearance and their core message.

But fear not, for the solution is as accessible as it is effective. The key lies in understanding the language of clothing and grooming and using it to reinforce, rather than undermine, your message. This approach involves selecting attire that resonates with your audience, embodies the essence of your message, and aligns with the context of the interaction.

To implement this strategy, start by researching the expectations and norms of your audience. Are you addressing corporate executives or creative artists? Will you be under the scrutiny of a conservative panel or engaging with a tech-savvy crowd? Each scenario demands a different sartorial dialect.

Once the context is clear, curate your wardrobe accordingly. Choose pieces that are clean, well-fitted, and appropriate for the occasion. Attention to detail is paramount—ensure that your clothing is free of wrinkles and stains, and that your shoes are polished. Personal grooming should mirror this meticulousness; a neat hairstyle, trimmed nails, and subtle fragrance can go a long way in crafting a polished image.

The effectiveness of this approach is not merely anecdotal. Studies in social psychology have consistently demonstrated the impact of a speaker's appearance on their perceived credibility and persuasiveness. When aligned with the expectations of the audience, a speaker's attire can enhance their authority and the receptiveness of their message.

But what of alternative solutions? After all, one might argue that true merit should transcend superficial appearances. Indeed, fostering an environment that values content over form is a noble endeavor. However, until such paradigms shift universally, the pragmatic approach is to master the existing rules of the game.

One alternative is to focus solely on the content of the message, hoping that its strength will shine through regardless of appearance. While this can be effective in certain contexts, it often requires an already established reputation or an exceptionally compelling message to overcome initial visual judgments.

Another approach might be to deliberately subvert expectations with a unique or unconventional appearance to make a statement. This can be powerful when done intentionally and in alignment with the message, but it carries the risk of overshadowing the content or alienating the audience.

In the end, dressing for success is not about vanity or superficiality; it's about acknowledging the role that appearance plays in communication and leveraging it to amplify your message. It's about understanding that in the intricate dance of conveying ideas, every element—from the precision of your words to the cut of your suit—plays a part in the grand performance.

So, as you stand before your next audience, remember that your attire is whispering long before you start to speak. Make sure it's echoing the very essence of your message, paving the way for your words to resonate with clarity and conviction. After all, in the theatre of human interaction, every detail contributes to your deliverance.

5.5 Managing Stage Presence

In the realm of public speaking, commanding the stage is akin to a conductor leading an orchestra. Each movement, each pause, and each inflection plays a part in the symphony of your speech. With this in mind, the goal of our expedition is to create a dynamic stage presence that captivates and maintains audience engagement from the first word to the final bow.

Embarking on this journey requires a few essentials: a willingness to step out of your comfort zone, an understanding of your personal speaking style, and a commitment to continuous improvement. You'll need to refine your nonverbal communication skills—gestures, facial expressions, and posture—as well as your vocal delivery. Visual aids and props may also play a role, depending on your context.

Imagine, for a moment, a map laid out before you, each landmark representing a step in mastering your stage presence. At the outset, you see the broad path ahead: understanding your audience, developing a strong opening, sustaining interest, utilizing space effectively, and delivering a memorable close.

Let us now traverse the intricate landscape of these steps. Picture your audience, a sea of faces waiting to be led on a journey. How do you captivate them from the get-go? Begin with a powerful opening—a startling fact, a poignant story, or a thought-provoking question. "Have you ever wondered what it takes to truly command attention?" This invites listeners into your narrative, sparking their curiosity.

As you delve deeper into your discourse, maintain a rhythmic stance with your words. Like a heart pulsing life through the veins, your sentence structure—short, sharp phrases punctuated by longer, more contemplative ones—creates a dynamic pace that keeps the audience's attention.

A few tips to enhance your performance: employ the power of the pause, giving your words space to reverberate. Use eye contact to connect personally with audience members, creating a bond that extends beyond the footlights.

But beware, for pitfalls abound. Overuse of gestures can distract, and monotone delivery can induce lethargy. To verify your success, look for nods, note-taking, or laughter—signs that your audience is engaged. If eyes are wandering or phones are emerging, recalibrate and recapture their focus.

Should you encounter disengagement, do not despair. Troubleshooting is part of the process. Perhaps your stories lack relevance, or your voice fails to reach the back of the room. Adjust your volume, slow your pace, or inject a dose of humour to rekindle the dwindling flame of attention.

Remember, the stage is both your canvas and your arena. Stride with purpose, gesture with intent, and speak with conviction. Let your presence fill the space, reaching out to envelop your audience in the embrace of your narrative.

Consider the silent power of your posture. Stand tall, shoulders back, exuding confidence. Yet, allow yourself moments of vulnerability, for it is in these that true connection is forged. "Can you recall a time when you felt truly heard? "Honestly, a quick introspection should critically motivate you to enhance your persona to strike a better bond between speaker and listener.

In the dance of dialogue, your attire has already set the stage, but your movement and voice now carry the melody. They must harmonize with your message, ensuring that your physicality and vocal expression amplify, rather than detract from, your words.

As the final note of your speech lingers in the air, leave your audience with a lasting message. A compelling call to action, a provocative thought, or a heartfelt thank you can be the encore that etches your performance in their memories.

Summing up, managing stage presence is an art form that blends the visual with the verbal, the physical with the psychological. It is a craft that demands practice, reflection, and a touch of bravery. As you close the back cover of this guide, may you step onto your next stage emboldened, equipped not just with techniques, but with the spirit of a performer ready to transform the stage into a realm of endless possibility.

CHAPTER 6

THE SCIENCE OF STORYTELLING

"Storytelling is the most powerful way to put ideas into the world today."

Robert McKee

6.1 Elements of a Compelling Story

In the realm of storytelling, there are core threads that weave together to form the rich tapestry of a narrative that resonates with its audience. Every story, whether whispered by the flickering campfire or broadcasted across the digital cosmos, relies on fundamental elements to captivate and engage. As we embark on this exploration, let's first outline the elements that are the backbone of a compelling narrative, before delving into the intricacies that give each tale its unique pulse.

As we set the stage for our in-depth analysis, it is crucial to recognize these elements as the keystones in the arch of storytelling. They are the silent beats that, when orchestrated with skill, create a symphony that lingers in the mind long after the last page is turned.

The essential components of a compelling story include:

1. Relatable Characters
2. Immersive Settings
3. Engaging Plot
4. Purposeful Conflict
5. Emotional Depth
6. Thematic Significance
7. Satisfying Resolution

With these pillars in mind, let us delve deeper.

Relatable Characters

The heart of any story beats within its characters. They are the vessels through which we experience the journey, their desires and fears becoming our own. When characters mirror the complexities of real life, readers find themselves reflected in the story, creating a bond that is both profound and personal. Consider Elizabeth Bennet's wit and resilience in "Pride and Prejudice," or Harry Potter's unyielding courage in the face of darkness, or

Rehmat's character in Kabuliwala – their stories endure because they are characters who breathe, bleed, and aspire as we do.

What, then, makes a character relatable? It is a delicate blend of flaw and virtue, the layered backstory, and the humanity that shines through in their actions and choices. When readers witness a character struggle and grow, they too feel a part of that transformation.

Evidence of this can be seen in countless testimonials from readers who see themselves in the plights and triumphs of their beloved protagonists. Memoirs of overcoming adversity, such as Maya Angelou's "I Know Why the Caged Bird Sings," resonate with audiences because of the raw authenticity of the author's character portrayal. Or still, the impact of cinema in Indian society in terms of relatable characters like Viru and Jay of the famous epic movie 'Sholay.'

In practice, consider the art of creating a character profile, not merely listing traits but understanding the character's history, motivations, and potential evolution. It is through these profiles that writers can craft beings of ink and imagination that leap off the page and into the hearts of readers.

Immersive Settings

Have you ever lost yourself in the winding streets of a fictional city, or yearned for the scent of a pine forest that exists only within the boundaries of a book? The setting of a story is more than a backdrop; it is the canvas upon which all action is painted. It shapes the narrative, influences characters, and can become as iconic as the protagonists themselves. The misty moors of "Wuthering Heights" or the dynamic character of Anandi with the varying shades of social nuances by Munshi Premchand is but a prolific example of immersive settings.

Crafting an immersive setting requires a keen eye for detail and a deep understanding of the world one wishes to create. It is not simply about elaborate descriptions but about choosing the right details that evoke the essence of a place. A single, well-placed image, like the green light at the end of Daisy's dock, can symbolize an entire thematic undercurrent.

Testimonials from bestselling authors often cite travel, research, and personal experience as invaluable tools in creating settings that readers can step into. Similarly, a public speaker must draw inferences from his own experiences and perceptions to make his story relatable.

Engaging Plot

What is a story without the ebb and flow of events that keep us turning pages long into the night? An engaging plot is the spine of the narrative, each vertebra is a carefully crafted scene that supports the weight of the whole. It is a journey with a clear direction, yet filled with enough twists and turns to surprise and delight. Consider the intricate dance of intrigue in "Game of Thrones" or the relentless pace of "The Da Vinci Code."

To construct a plot that ensnares the reader, one must balance the familiar with the unexpected, weaving threads that connect in unforeseen ways. It is the art of foreshadowing, the skill of pacing, and the mastery of tension and release that creates a plot that thrums with energy. Famous satirist in Hindi literature – Krishn Chandra's story of 'Jamun Ka Ped' was an exaggerated yet poignant comment on the social structure of its time.

Purposeful Conflict

Conflict is the crucible in which character is tested, and from which the story's true essence emerges. It is the clash of desires, the obstacle that seems insurmountable, the question that begs an answer. Without conflict, there is no change, no arc, no story. It is the lifeblood of narrative, pumping tension and drive into every scene. Whether it's the internal struggle within Hamlet or the epic battles in "The Lord of the Rings," conflict propels the story forward and keeps us invested.

But what makes conflict purposeful? It must be deeply rooted in the characters and the world they inhabit. It should challenge their beliefs, force them to grow, and ultimately lead to a transformation that is both earned and satisfying. As enacted by Amitabh Bachchan's portrayal of an angry man in the famous art form (cinema) Zanjir. Yet again, evidence of the power of conflict can be found in the countless stories that have stood the test of time, tales that hinge on the resolution of profound and compelling strife.

Emotional Depth

A story that moves us is a story that stays with us. Emotional depth is the element that allows readers to experience the joys, sorrows, and fears of the characters as if they were their own. It is what makes a story resonate on a personal level, creating a lasting impact. The cathartic release in "To Kill a Mockingbird" or the poignant longing in the story 'Kabuliwala' by Rabindra Nath Tagore exemplifies emotional depths in storytelling.

To evoke genuine emotions amongst the audience, a writer and speaker must be willing to delve into the complexities of the human heart, to explore the nuances of feeling and the shadows of motive. It is a careful balancing act, offering enough to stir empathy without descending into sentimentality.

Testimonials from audiences often highlight moments in history that have brought them to tears or laughter, scenes that have remained etched in their memory because of the emotions they evoked as the inspiring and motivating Nehru's speech 'Tryst with Destiny' at the midnight hour of the Indian Independence.

Thematic Significance

A story may entertain, but a story with thematic significance challenges, questions, and offers insights into the human condition. It is the underlying message, the moral or question that lingers after the final page is turned. Whether it is the exploration of power in "1984" or the commentary on social class in the movie "Lagan," by Amir Khan gives stories their weight and relevance.

To weave thematic significance into a narrative, a speaker must understand what they wish to convey, the larger conversation into which their story enters. It requires a depth of thought and a willingness to engage with complex ideas.

Satisfying Resolution

The final note of any story is its resolution – the culmination of all that has come before. It is the moment when conflicts are resolved, questions are answered, and the reader is allowed to exhale. A satisfying resolution does not necessarily mean a happy ending, but it should feel true to the story and its characters. The bitter sweet finale of 'The Post Office' by Tagore reflects the resolution and honour of a narrative journey. Crafting a satisfying resolution means understanding the expectations set by the story, tying up loose ends, and leaving the reader with a sense of completion.

As we transition from one point to the next, it is important to remember that these elements are not isolated; they are interconnected, each enriching the other. A relatable character is grounded in an immersive setting; a purposeful conflict drives an engaging plot; emotional depth adds resonance to thematic significance; and a satisfying resolution brings closure to the journey.

In exploring the elements of a compelling story, we find that it is not simply about following a formula, but about understanding the alchemy of narrative. It is about crafting a tale that whispers to the soul, mirrors the complexity of life, and ultimately, reminds us of our shared humanity.

As you reflect on these elements, consider the stories that have stayed with you, and that have changed you. What was it about those narratives that captured your heart and mind? How can you, as a storyteller, create worlds that others will not want to leave? These are the questions that drive us to the page, to the endless pursuit of the perfect story and their deliverance.

6.2 Structuring Your Narrative

Embarking on the journey of structuring your narrative, you're met with the daunting task of not just telling a story, but telling it well. A story that flows, entrances, and retains its hold on the reader long after the final period is placed requires meticulous design. You aspire to achieve such a feat, and the path lies before you, ready to be unravelled, step by step.

Imagine the satisfaction of seeing your narrative unfold just as you envisioned, with readers immersed in the world you've created, clinging to every word. This is your goal: to construct a narrative that's as engaging in its structure as it is in its storytelling.

Before you embark on this architectural venture, ensure you're equipped with the right tools. You will need a clear understanding of your story's theme and message, a detailed outline of the plot, comprehensive character profiles, and a richly imagined setting. Equally important are a quiet workspace, dedication to the craft, and, perhaps most crucially, the perseverance to see the project through to its end.

Let's begin with a broad overview. The structure of your narrative should encompass the introduction of your world and characters, an inciting incident that sets the plot in motion, rising action filled with conflict and character development, a climactic peak, followed by the falling action, and finally, a resolution that leaves your readers satisfied yet possibly yearning for more.

Delving deeper, we must dissect these elements. Your introduction should be an enticing invitation, a subtle seduction that whispers of the wonders within. Here, you plant the seeds of your world, introduce the protagonist, and set the stage for the inciting incident, which will catapult your characters into action.

As tension builds, your characters will face challenges that test their mettle, and it's within these trials that their true natures are revealed. The plot must ascend steadily, with each conflict more harrowing than the last, until the climax crashes over your narrative like a wave, leaving in its wake the falling action and the threads that need tying.

But how does one ensure that this ascent is neither too steep nor too gentle? Through the careful pacing of events and the strategic placement of peaks and valleys in the narrative, you create a rhythm that pulsates with life. Think of your favourite novel, the way it didn't just capture your attention but held it captive, the pacing a masterful command that you could not, and would not, break away from.

Intersperse your narrative with moments of introspection, allowing your characters, and through them, your readers, to breathe, ponder, and grow. Offer tips such as the importance of character arcs that mirror the plot's progression, and warnings against the pitfalls of pacing that lurches or lags.

How do you know when your structural endeavours have succeeded? The testing or validation comes from the visceral reaction of your audience and their applause and feedback.

Yet, even the best-laid plans can encounter snags. When faced with a narrative thread that tangles or a character that refuses to comply, troubleshoot by stepping back and viewing your story from a fresh perspective. Perhaps an anecdote requires pruning or a character's motivation needs refining. Address these issues with patience and creativity, and your story will find its way back on course.

Remember to vary your sentence openers, to keep the prose dynamic and alive. A narrative that dances with variety will engage your audience more effectively than one that drones in monotony. Paint your scenes with vivid imagery, letting the hues of your words colour the imagination of your audience. Invite them to taste the salt on the sea breeze, to feel the cobblestones beneath their feet, and to hear the whisper of the willow leaves in the gentle night or feel the extreme cold temperatures of adventurous difficulties.

Engage your readers with direct questions, drawing them deeper into the narrative of characters' relevance, validity, and authenticity. Such questions are not simply heard; they are felt, pondered, and answered in the silent chambers of the reader's mind.

Craft your sentences with precision, choosing the most potent verbs and the most evocative nouns, allowing adverbs and adjectives to play supporting roles rather than lead. When a particular point demands attention, lay emphasis with correct pauses and intonation.

In your pursuit of clarity and impact, favour simple language. There is an elegance in simplicity that often surpasses the convoluted, and it is in understanding that your listener finds a connection. Listen to the rhythm and cadence of your words, for they are the heartbeat of your narrative, the pulse that either quickens with excitement or calms with reflection. When appropriate, integrate quotations or dialogues to lend authenticity and variety. Allow your characters to speak for themselves, their voices distinct and resonant.

When etching a story and webbing it into a speech you are not merely an architect, a sculptor, or a weaver of dreams but a guide for those who are on a journey with you in a shared experience leading to a common destination.

6.3 Creating Emotional Impact

In the realm of storytelling, the true resonance of a tale lies not solely in its plot or characters, but in its capacity to evoke emotions from the audience. As a freelance consultant with an extensive background in narrative design, I have witnessed first-hand the transformative power of a well-told story. Herein, I will dissect a particular instance where emotional impact was paramount, and the techniques employed to achieve it.

Set in the bustling heart of New York City, an environment ripe with stories, my case study revolves around a keynote speech delivered at a prestigious conference on the future of technology. The backdrop was an auditorium filled with industry experts, innovators, and a palpable sense of expectation.

The central figure was a young entrepreneur who had developed an application that harnessed the power of virtual reality for educational purposes. While the product was groundbreaking, it was the emotional core of the presentation that captivated the audience.

The speaker faced a significant challenge: how to communicate the value of application in a way that transcended the technical jargon and struck a chord with the audience. It was needed to make the audience feel the potential impact of the work.

The approach selected was a narrative woven into the speech, recounting the story of a child from a developing country who had never stepped foot in a classroom. Through the application, this child was able to explore the cosmos, dive into the depths of the ocean, and walk amongst the dinosaurs. The narrative was punctuated by the speaker's childhood memories of the grandmother, who had instilled a lifelong love for learning.

The results were palpable. The audience was visibly moved, many to the brink of tears, as they experienced the journey of the child and the passion of the speaker. Data from post-event surveys showed that the presentation was rated as the most impactful of the conference, with numerous attendees expressing a desire to learn more about this application.

Upon reflection, the success of the speech could be attributed to the emotional connection that was forged. While other competitors focused on specs and statistics, the speaker in question told a story that illustrated the human element of the technology. However, one might argue that the reliance on pathos could overshadow the practical aspects of the product. This criticism, though valid, does not diminish the effectiveness of the emotional appeal.

To enhance the audience's understanding, visual aids were used sparingly but effectively. A short video clip showed the child's joy as he interacted with the virtual world, a stark contrast to his reality.

This example of personal narrative was a microcosm of the larger theme of the conference: the potential for technology to change lives. It was demonstrated that innovation, at its core, is about improving the human condition and emotional connect.

The speech concluded with a thought that lingered in the air, a question posed directly to the audience: "What if the key to unlocking the world's potential was not in our technology, but in our humanity?"

As you read this account, consider how you might employ similar techniques in your storytelling. Can you recall a moment when a story, perhaps even a simple anecdote, changed your perspective?

Narrative is a vessel for emotion, and emotion is the currency of connection. In my work, I have seen the profound impact that a story can have when it is crafted with intention. Whether through the lens of a child learning beyond his confines or an entrepreneur pitching their life's work, the thread that binds us is unmistakably human.

So friends, when crafting your narrative, seek out the heartbeat of the story. Is it nestled in the courage of your protagonist? Or perhaps it is hidden in the quiet determination of your antagonist. Find it, and let it pulse through every word and image you create.

In the art of storytelling, we are reminded that to evoke emotion is to speak to the soul. It is to reach into the collective experiences of our humanity and touch something universal. So, I urge you, as you pen your narratives, to remember the power of a story well told. For it is in the heart of the story that the true emotional impact lies.

6.4 The Role of Conflict

In the intricate mosaic of storytelling, the pulse that quickens the audience's heart and draws them into the narrative is often the drumbeat of conflict. It's a force that propels the plot and moulds characters, shaping the journey that keeps readers, listeners, or viewers tethered to the edge of their seats. Understanding this dynamic element is not a mere academic exercise but an exploration of the very core of human engagement.

As we delve into the world of conflict, certain terms become beacons that illuminate our path. A term like 'antagonist' not only identifies a character but also encapsulates a force that opposes our hero. Similarly, 'climax' transcends its common usage, marking the zenith of struggle where opposing forces collide with the greatest intensity. These are not just words; they are the scaffolding upon which the architecture of a compelling story is built.

To appreciate the nuances of storytelling, one must first become acquainted with the lexicon of conflict. These terms include protagonist, antagonist, conflict, internal conflict, external conflict, stakes, resolution, and climax. Each of these holds a world of meaning that, when understood, can transform a mundane speech into a riveting tale that echoes long after the last word is spoken.

Let us begin with the protagonist, the central figure of our story. This character is not merely the focal point but also the one whom the audience accompanies on the journey, whose eyes become their own. The protagonist's desires, fears, and actions become the substance of the narrative.

Opposing the protagonist is the antagonist, a character or force that presents hurdles and injects tension into the tale. The antagonist's role is not to be vilified but to serve as a catalyst for the protagonist's growth, pushing them towards their limits.

When we speak of conflict, we refer to the struggle between the protagonist and the antagonist. But conflict is a chameleon, taking on various forms. It can be as overt as a war or as subtle as a character's internal battle with self-doubt.

Internal conflict, that gnawing turmoil within a character, can be as gripping as any external skirmish. It is the silent war waged in the recesses of the mind, where the outcome can redefine a character's essence.

External conflict, on the other hand, is the outward clash with forces beyond the character's control. From natural disasters to societal expectations, these conflicts shape the physical journey of the story.

Stakes are the currency of empathy. They answer the question of 'why should we care?' by defining what the protagonist stands to lose or gain. High stakes amplify tension and investment in the story's outcome.

The resolution brings the promise of closure, the tying up of narrative threads that satiate the audience's desire for completion. It is where the chaos of conflict finds order.

The climax is the crescendo of conflict, the moment of highest tension where the protagonist and antagonist confront their ultimate trial. This peak not only decides the fate of the characters but also delivers the story's most profound emotional impact.

In the real world, these concepts find their counterparts. The protagonist is akin to the underdog whose story we champion, the antagonist mirrors the challenges we face in our own lives. Internal conflict is the self-doubt that whispers in our ears before a public speech, while external conflict resembles the obstacles that life unpredictably throws at us.

The stakes echo the risks we take in pursuit of our dreams, and the resolution reflects our longing for peace after turmoil. The climax can be seen in the pivotal moments of our lives when we must make defining choices.

Take, for example, the entrepreneur who must decide between a secure job and starting their own business. The stakes are high, the internal conflict palpable, and the climax dramatic. This real-world scenario is rife with the elements of storytelling conflict, rendering it a tale in its own right.

In harnessing these concepts for your speeches, you transform the podium into a stage, the audience into fellow travellers, and the message into an odyssey. Conflict, when wielded with skill, becomes more than a literary device—it becomes the heartbeat of engagement.

When next you stand to deliver a speech, consider the elements of conflict. Envision your audience not just as passive recipients but as engaged participants in a journey you craft with every word you utter. Remember, the power of your message lies not just in the information conveyed but in the emotional resonance that the journey of conflict imbues.

6.5 Anecdotes That Stick

In the warm glow of a campfire, a group of travellers from disparate corners of the earth huddled together, their faces illuminated by the flickering light. Among them was an old man, his hair as white as the mountain peaks that loomed in the distance. His eyes sparkled with the wisdom of experience as he began to weave a tale that would captivate and linger in the minds of his audience long after the night had surrendered to dawn.

There was a young girl in his story, a spirited soul named Lila, who had an uncanny ability to capture the essence of life's moments in her tales. Her stories weren't just recitations of events but vivid experiences that painted the world in the hues of her emotions. Lila's words could make you feel the stifling heat of a summer's day or the biting cold of a winter storm. She had the rare gift of turning the mundane into the magical, and through her eyes, a simple walk in the market could become an epic adventure.

As the old man's story unfolded, it was clear that every detail was chosen with intention, each description crafted to draw the listeners deeper into Lila's world. The market was not just a place but a cacophony of colours, sounds, and scents. The spices in the air mixed with the tang of citrus, while the clamour of bargaining voices rose and fell like a symphony.

The travellers around the fire could almost feel themselves walking beside Lila and could sense her excitement as she encountered a street performer whose dance seemed to defy the very laws of physics. This was the emotional echo of the story, the connection that turned listeners into participants, making Lila's joys and discoveries their own.

But as with all good tales, there came an unexpected turn. Lila, in her quest to find the perfect narrative, stumbled upon a truth that was as unsettling as it was enlightening. The performer, the one who had danced with the grace of the wind, was doing so not to entertain but to distract the crowd from the pickpockets weaving through them. This revelation hit Lila like a cold wave, and it struck the listeners too, a surprising twist that mirrored the unpredictability of the anecdotes that stick.

The old man's story, while personal and unique, tapped into something universal—the realization that not all is as it seems and that wisdom often comes from looking beyond the surface. This was the universal truth at the heart of the old man's anecdote, a truth that resonated with every traveller by the fire, regardless of their origin.

"Do you see?" the old man asked, his voice a gentle nudge in the quiet that had befallen the group. "The best unforgettable stories are the ones that present us with a lens through which we can perceive the world in a new light. They are the ones that surprise us, that connect with us on a deeper level, and that reveal a wisdom we can apply in our own lives."

Indeed, the old man promised more than just a story; he promised a reflection of life itself, an assurance that within the pages of 'Anecdotes That Stick,' readers would find valuable insights and revelations. He enticed them with the prospect of learning how to select and deliver anecdotes that would not only reinforce their message but would also remain with their audience, becoming a part of their narrative tapestry.

Dear reader, have you ever found yourself entranced by a story, only to forget it as life rushes back in? Have you wondered what makes some tales cling to memory while others slip away? As a freelance consultant, I've seen the power of a well-told anecdote to transform presentations, to make messages resonate and stick.

With each chapter of this book, I invite you to delve deeper into the art of storytelling. You will learn not just to tell a story but to craft an experience that will stay with your audience long after the final words have been spoken. You will discover how to find the extraordinary in the ordinary, how to weave emotion into a narrative, and how to turn the unexpected into the unforgettable.

Let me ask you, what tales will you tell? What anecdotes will you share that will echo in the minds of your listeners, becoming a part of their own stories? The answers, I believe, await you in the journey we are about to embark upon together in the pages of 'Anecdotes That Stick.'

So, shall we begin?

CHAPTER 7

HARNESSING HUMOUR

"You may not be able to change a situation, but with humour you can change your attitude about it."

Allen Klein

7.1 Understanding Humour in Communication

Laughter amplifies through the air, an invisible connect between the speaker and listener, a mutual understanding that something amusing has been shared. But what is this intangible force that can bridge gaps and form bonds? Humour, a term so commonly used yet intricately complex, is the main subject we delve into now.

Humour, in its simplest definition, is the quality of being amusing or comic, particularly as expressed in literature or speech. It's the spark that ignites laughter and the glue that can hold an audience's rapt attention. To further clarify, humour is not just a joke or a witty line; it's a multifaceted tool that encompasses timing, context, and the shared knowledge between the communicator and the audience.

As we explore the key elements of humour, it's important to recognize that it operates on various levels. There's the surface level of slapstick and visual gags, straightforward and often universally understood. Then there's the deeper, more intellectual humour that might play on words, cultural references, or societal observations. This layered approach allows humour to be tailored to different audiences and to serve different purposes.

While the exact origins of humour are as elusive as the concept itself, we can trace its role in communication back to ancient times. Philosophers like Plato and Aristotle pondered over the mechanics and ethics of humour. Fast forward to the modern era, and the study of humour has become a field of its own, with psychologists and linguists analysing why and how it works.

Contextualized within a broader framework, humour serves as a powerful instrument in communication, cutting through tension, building relationships, and enhancing messages. Whether it's a politician using a witty remark to ease into a difficult topic or a teacher employing a funny anecdote to make a lesson more memorable, humour has a place in nearly all forms of human interaction.

Real-world applications of humour are vast and varied. In marketing, a clever punchline can make an advertisement stick in the minds of consumers. In motivational speeches, a light-hearted story can inspire and engage an audience, making the message more palatable and the speaker more relatable.

However, common misconceptions about humour abound. It is often mistaken as a tool only for entertainment, overlooking its potential for influence and education. Similarly, humour is not universally translatable; what is humorous in one culture or setting may not be in another, leading to misinterpretations that can hinder rather than help communication.

With these nuances in mind, consider the subtlety required to effectively wield humour. The most adept communicators are those who can read their audience, understanding not only the collective mood but also the cultural and social nuances that will shape how humour is received.

Why do we laugh when we do, and why does that laughter sometimes fail to materialize? It's a dance of context, delivery, and reception, a trifecta that, when aligned, produces the magical sound of laughter. But it's not enough to simply know that humour can make a difference; understanding how to craft it thoughtfully is the key to truly engaging and impacting an audience.

Employing humour, therefore, is a delicate balance. It requires a deep understanding of language, a keen sense of timing, and, perhaps most importantly, a genuine connection with people. "A day without laughter is a day wasted," Charlie Chaplin once said, reminding us of the inherent value found in those moments of shared amusement.

In conclusion, as we navigate the art and science of humour in communication, it's evident that its role extends far beyond mere entertainment. It's a strategic tool that, when mastered, can elevate discourse, cement connections, and, ultimately, illuminate the human experience. Through humour, we find common ground, and in that common ground, we find understanding. Just then I am reminded of the famous quote of Charles Dickens "There is nothing in the world so irresistibly contagious as laughter and good humour".

7.2 Timing and Delivery

In the delicate art of communication, few skills are more nuanced than the mastery of timing and delivery, especially when humour is involved. This mastery ensures that the humour lands effectively, enhancing rather than detracting from the message at hand. But how exactly does one navigate the intricate play of comedic timing? It's a question that has puzzled performers, speakers, and writers alike for centuries.

Central to the theme of this exploration is the assertion that the successful integration of humour into any form of communication relies heavily on the precise timing and delivery of the content. To understand this, let's delve into the mechanics of what makes the humour tick.

A comedic mastermind once compared humour to music, suggesting that the timing of a joke is akin to the rhythm of a song. It is the first piece of evidence that we encounter when examining the impact of the humour. Much like a well-timed beat drop in a musical performance, a joke must land at the exact moment when the audience's anticipation peaks, but before their attention wanes. This critical synchrony can elicit laughter, or in its absence, the joke may fall flat, and its potential for connection is lost.

To dive deeper into this evidence, consider the physiological response to laughter. Scientific studies reveal that the brain's limbic system, which controls emotions, is activated when humour is processed. The timing of a joke triggers a cognitive process that anticipates a humorous payoff, creating a sense of pleasure when the punchline is delivered just right. This reaction is not just psychological; it's a physical experience that can bond the speaker and listener in a moment of shared levity.

However, there are counterarguments to the importance of timing and delivery. Some argue that the content of humour itself—the wit, the irony, the clever twist of words—is enough to provoke laughter, irrespective of when and how it's delivered. A brilliantly constructed joke, they say, stands on its merit and can withstand variations in timing like the famous character of Charlie Chaplin, master of combining humour with time.

Yet, a rebuttal to this viewpoint emerges from the realm of stand-up comedy, where the same joke can elicit uproarious laughter or awkward silence based solely on the comedian's control over timing and delivery. The same words, spoken with a different cadence or inflected with a unique intonation, can yield vastly different reactions. It's the performer's acute awareness of the audience's mood and the immediacy of the environment that informs the precise moment the joke is unveiled.

Further supporting evidence for the significance of timing comes from the world of cinema. Editors and directors work meticulously to ensure that comedic scenes are cut in such a way that the timing of visual gags or lines of dialogue maximizes their humorous impact. The slightest miscalculation can disrupt the comedic flow, proving that even in a scripted and rehearsed setting, timing is paramount. A classical example is the character of Raju in the iconic movie 'Mera Naam Joker'.

As we draw this discussion to a close, let's not forget the vital role that delivery plays in the comedic equation. The right words, at the right moment, spoken with the wrong inflection, can render a joke ineffective. It's the marriage of timing and delivery that truly allows humour to resonate, transcend mere words, and become an experience that connects us.

In conclusion, the assertion that mastering timing and delivery is essential for humour to enhance communication holds true. Through precise control and keen awareness of the audience, a speaker can transform a simple message into an engaging and memorable interaction. It is this mastery that allows humour to fulfil its potential as a powerful tool for connection, a means to not only entertain but also to enlighten and persuade. As we continue to explore the complexities of humour in the chapters that follow, remember that at its heart, it is the human connection that we seek—a connection that is made all the stronger by the laughter we share. So truly said by Victor Borge "Laughter is the shortest distance between two people".

7.3 Appropriateness and Cultural Sensitivity

In an ever-shrinking world, where cultures collide and mingle with increasing frequency, humour's role as a social lubricant is tested by its capacity to either unite or divide. The global village is no joke, and as creators and communicators, we tread a thin line between eliciting laughter and causing offense. Such is the maze in which we find ourselves, deciphering the appropriateness of humour and its cultural sensitivity—or, at times, insensitivity.

Picture this: a bustling market in a distant land, where spices scent the air and a polyglot of voices rise in a cacophony of life. There, humour is the currency of connection, but it's a currency whose value fluctuates wildly across the map. What elicits a hearty laugh in one corner of the world might be met with stony silence—or worse, a furrowed brow of consternation—in another. The problem, then, is clear: how do we ensure that our attempts at humour translate across the diverse tapestry of human culture without losing their charm or, more importantly, without disrespecting their audience?

Consider the consequences of ignoring the cultural context in which humour is delivered. A joke that plays on stereotypes—however benign the intent—may perpetuate harmful prejudices, widening the chasm between 'us' and 'them'. A misstep in this delicate dance can sour relationships, tarnish reputations, and even spark diplomatic incidents. The ripple effect of a single ill-considered jest can be far-reaching, damaging the very fibres of social harmony.

But what of the solution? How do we navigate this complex landscape? The answer begins with empathy and education. To be effective purveyors of humour, we must first become students of the cultures we wish to entertain. This calls for a willingness to listen, to understand, and to appreciate the nuances of different societal norms and values. It requires research, reflection, and a touch of humility. Only then can we craft humour that resonates on a universal frequency, laughter that builds bridges rather than burns them.

Implementing this approach involves several steps. Firstly, we must engage with the culture, not as outsiders looking in, but as active participants. This immersion provides insight into the subtleties of what is considered humourous and what is not. Next, we must vet our material with members of the culture in question—trusted individuals who can guide us away from potential pitfalls. Furthermore, we must be prepared to iterate, to refine our humour based on feedback, ensuring that it aligns with the sensibilities of our audience.

Evidence of the effectiveness of this tactful approach can be seen in the work of comedians and writers who have successfully crossed cultural barriers. They have done so not by diluting their humour but by tailoring it to their audiences with respect and intelligence. They prove that laughter need not be lost in translation and that with the right touch, humour can be a universal language. Mrs Funnybones by Twinkle Khanna is one such example that fits the bill.

Are there alternate solutions? Certainly. One might consider avoiding culturally specific humour altogether, opting instead for themes that are universally human—an approach that minimizes risk but also, perhaps, the richness of the comedic tapestry. Another option is to maintain a dynamic dialogue with the audience, allowing their reactions to guide the evolution of the humour. This creates a collaborative environment where humour is shaped not just by the comedian or writer but by the cultural context itself.

In this intricate ballet of words and witticisms, what stands out is the profound power of laughter. It is a power that can unite us in our shared humanity, but only if wielded with care and consideration. As we move forward, let us not shy away from the challenge but embrace it, crafting humour that celebrates our differences while acknowledging the common ground on which we all stand. In the end, it is not just about the jokes we tell, but the understanding and respect they convey, that will echo in the halls of our collective memory.

7.4 The Risks and Rewards of Self-Deprecation

Self-deprecation is a form of humour that involves belittling oneself through modest or depreciative remarks. It's a tightrope walk above a chasm of potential misunderstandings and a meadow of endearment. A comedian might quip about their own quirks, an executive might jest about a minor oversight, or a friend might downplay their own achievements. These moments, when crafted with care, can disarm, charm, and foster relatability. Yet, when misjudged, they can undermine authority and elicit discomfort. This exploration delves into the artful balancing act of self-deprecating humour.

Imagine walking into a room where the walls are adorned with mirrors reflecting every angle. This room is akin to the realm of self-deprecation—every remark is a reflection of oneself, for better or for worse. Why tread such a reflective path? The root of this strategy is to humanize oneself, to break the ice and bridge gaps between individuals of differing statuses, or to punctuate a narrative with humility.

But what grounds do we have to tread here? What benchmarks can we set to navigate this landscape? The criteria for effective self-deprecation are context, audience, intent, and frequency. These elements provide the framework for a balanced analysis of when this comedic tool enhances rapport and when it risks undermining one's persona.

Through the lens of these criteria, consider the similarities between a seasoned politician who jests about their dancing skills and a CEO who laughs off a minor typo in a presentation. Both instances use self-deprecation to appear more accessible and human. They share a purpose: to connect with their audience by showcasing a touch of vulnerability.

Yet, when we shine a light on their differences, the nuances begin to emerge. A politician's self-deprecating joke on a personal quirk can be disarming and endearing, fostering a sense of shared human experience. On the other hand, a Leader repeatedly making light of business errors, however small, might inadvertently signal incompetence or a lack of seriousness. The stark contrast here lies in the stakes and the realm each individual operates within.

Visual aids, like a graph with a humour index on one axis and credibility on the other, can clearly illustrate the inverse relationship that often exists between the two, dependent on the factors mentioned. As the use of self-deprecating humour increases, credibility can either plateau or decrease, if not handled with finesse.

Digging deeper, we uncover insights into the broader implications of this humour style. Effective self-deprecation requires self-awareness and timing. It's a strategic reveal of one's own imperfections in a controlled manner. When done well, it's a masterclass in humility and relatability, but when overplayed, it risks becoming a self-inflicted wound to one's reputation.

How does this translate into today's world? In the age of social media, where personal and professional boundaries blur, the use of self-deprecating humour by influencers or public figures can be a double-edged sword. It can make them seem more relatable to their followers, yet it can also become a tool for others to amplify their criticisms. The contemporary relevance of self-deprecation is thus tied to the digital stage upon which it unfolds.

Are we, then, to embrace or eschew self-deprecation? The answer is neither binary nor simple. It is about understanding the delicate interplay between self-awareness and public perception. It's about recognizing when a light-hearted jab at oneself can disarm a tense room or when it might be misconstrued as a sign of self-doubt.

To illustrate, let's consider an anecdote. A professor, known for their rigorous standards, begins a lecture with a humorous story about his struggle to understand a complex theorem during their student days. The laughter that follows is not at the professor's expense but shared in the humanity of the learning process. This anecdote serves as a testament to the power of well-placed self-deprecation to foster connection and empathy.

Indeed, the style of self-deprecating humour is intricate. Should we find ourselves offbeat, a recalibration is but a step away. As we navigate this dancefloor of discourse, we must remain attuned to the rhythm of our audience's responses. It is in this dynamic interplay that the true artistry of self-deprecation lies.

And so, we circle back to the mirrors in that room. Each reflection offers a choice like in a magic mirror room: to mock or to endear, to alienate or to embrace. As we gaze into these reflective surfaces, let us choose wisely, ensuring that our self-deprecating humour serves not to diminish but to enhance our shared human experience.

7.5 Using Humour to Diffuse Tension

In the arena of public speaking, the power of laughter is often underestimated. It can transform an atmosphere charged with apprehension into one of ease and camaraderie. As a freelance consultant, I have witnessed the transformative impact of humour firsthand. In this chapter, we delve into the intricacies of using humour to diffuse tension, a technique that, when deployed adeptly, can turn a rigid presentation into a memorable experience.

Imagine an auditorium brimming with anticipation, the air thick with the invisible weight of expectation. This setting forms the stage for our case study, a high-stakes technology conference where industry experts and novices alike congregate to share and absorb knowledge. The main player, a software developer named Dolly, was about to present a groundbreaking application to an audience of peers and potential investors. Dolly's challenge was to captivate and engage a diverse and discerning audience, some of whom held the power to determine the future of her project.

The core challenge arose when technical difficulties threw a wrench into the proceedings. Dolly's presentation, meticulously planned, was suddenly at the mercy of a malfunctioning projector. The tension in the room was palpable, a silence punctuated only by the hum of the struggling equipment.

Her approach was unorthodox yet brilliant. Instead of allowing frustration to take the helm, she pivoted with a quip about how her software could organize everything except, apparently, a cooperative projector. The room erupted in laughter and tension, dissolving as the shared frustration was acknowledged and was converted into a lighter atmosphere.

The results were twofold: the audience was now endeared to Julia, seeing her not just as a developer but as a relatable individual, and the brief interlude bought time for the technical issues to be resolved without the audience growing restless. When the projector flickered back to life, Dolly resumed her presentation with the audience now firmly on her side.

Upon reflection, the incident highlighted the importance of adaptability and the power of humour as a tool for connection. It wasn't simply about making people laugh; it was about transforming an unexpected obstacle into an opportunity to showcase resilience and relatability. No visual aids were needed to enhance the understanding of this moment; Her quick wit was the picture-perfect response to an unforeseen challenge.

Connecting this experience to the larger narrative, it's clear that humour can be an invaluable asset in a presenter's toolkit. It not only serves to lighten the mood but also to humanize the speaker, forging a bond with the audience that can be more impactful than the content of the presentation itself.

So, as we consider the role of humour in presentations, we're left with a thought: in moments of tension, can we find the courage to laugh at ourselves, to share a moment of levity with those around us? Perhaps, in these instances, humour is not just a deflection but a declaration of our shared humanity.

Using humour to diffuse tension is not merely about the punchline; it's about the shared experience that laughter creates. It's about the courage to be vulnerable, to turn a moment of potential embarrassment into one of connection. It's about the strategic use of levity to transform the energy of a room, to convert passive listeners into active participants who are emotionally invested in the narrative unfolding before them.

Dolly's experience is a testament to the effectiveness of humour when used judiciously. Her quick thinking did not detract from her expertise; rather, it showcased her ability to navigate the unpredictable seas of public speaking with grace and humour. This isn't to say that humour is a panacea for all public speaking challenges; rather, it is a powerful tool to be wielded with discernment and timing.

As we continue to explore the nuances of this tool, we must also consider its limitations. Not all tensions are ripe for humour, and not all audiences will respond in kind. It is the speaker's task to read the room, to sense the undercurrents of the collective mood, and to choose their moments with care.

The essence of using humour to diffuse tension lies in the recognition that our words have the power to shape the emotional landscape of our audience. A well-timed joke can bridge gaps, dismantle barriers, and illuminate the common threads that bind us. It can turn a stumbling block into a stepping stone, a moment of awkwardness into an opportunity for connection.

In conclusion, the art of using humour in presentations is a delicate dance—a choreography that balances wit with wisdom, spontaneity with strategy, and self-awareness with audience sensitivity. As we undertake this dance, let us lead with authenticity and a genuine desire to connect, for it is in these genuine moments that humour reveals its truest power.

Remember laughter is the language of the soul as said by Pablo Neruda.

P
R
A
C
T
I
C
E

CHAPTER 8

PRACTICAL APPLICATIONS AND PRACTICE

"The difference between ordinary and extraordinary is practice."

Vladimir Horowitz

8.1 Public Speaking Drills

Public speaking, the art of addressing a crowd, is a skill honed over time, shaped by practice, and polished through persistent effort. Each speaker embarks on a unique journey towards eloquence, yet certain exercises prove universally beneficial in mastering this craft. These drills are designed to enhance various facets of your public speaking, from enunciation to the art of captivating storytelling. Let this chapter serve as your guide, offering practical tools to elevate your oratorical prowess.

Imagine standing before an audience, the spotlight casting its glow upon you. Your heart beats in tandem with the hushed anticipation of the crowd. Here, within these pages, lies the key to transforming that moment from a daunting trial into a triumphant victory. So, lets begin?

Diction Enhancement

Breath Control and Vocal Resonance

Storytelling Mastery

Gestures and Body Language

Audience Engagement Techniques

Handling Stage Fright

The Craft of Persuasive Speech

8.1(a) Diction Enhancement

Clear articulation forms the cornerstone of effective public speaking. Each word should emerge crisp and intelligible, ensuring that your message is not only heard but understood.

Detail Expansion

To improve diction, start by reading aloud, focusing on enunciation. Articulate consonants, practice tongue twisters, and modulate your tone. Record your voice, listen back, and evaluate your clarity. Over time, your speech will become more precise, and your words more impactful.

Evidence and Testimonials

Renowned speakers, from Winston Churchill to Martin Luther King Jr and down to Shashi Tharoor understood the power of clear diction. Their speeches resonate across time, not just for the content, but for their impeccable delivery. Voice coaches emphasize its importance, citing improved diction as a driver for increased comprehension and retention among audiences.

Practical Applications

Incorporate diction exercises into your daily routine. Challenge yourself to articulate difficult passages from literature or speeches. Engage in conversations that push the boundaries of your vocabulary, and always seek feedback.

8.1(b) Breath Control and Vocal Resonance

To captivate an audience, a speaker's voice must resonate, carrying with it authority and emotion. Breath control is the invisible ally that empowers this resonance.

Detail Expansion

Practice deep breathing exercises to expand your lung capacity. Use your diaphragm to control airflow, and project your voice from within. Singing exercises can also fortify your vocal cords and enhance your capacity to sustain notes and modulate pitch.

Evidence and Testimonials

Opera singers are the epitome of breath control and vocal resonance. Their techniques, adapted for public speaking, can fill a room with sound, even without a microphone. Testimonials from experienced speakers corroborate the transformative effect of good breath control on public presence.

Practical Applications

Join a choir or take singing lessons. Regularly practice breathing exercises used by professional singers and speakers. Before a speech, warm up your voice and relax your breathing to prepare for a resonant delivery.

8.1(c) Storytelling Mastery

A story well told can capture hearts, change minds, and be remembered long after facts and figures fade away. Stories not only just enhance the captivating speech but build a strong connection with every listener in a personalised manner.

Detail Expansion

Develop your storytelling by crafting narratives that resonate with your audience. Use descriptive language to paint vivid scenes, build tension with pacing, and create relatable characters. Remember, every good story has a clear conflict and resolution.

Evidence and Testimonials

Great leaders, such as Barack Obama and the legendary Field Marshal Manekshaw often used stories to illustrate complex issues, making them relatable and understandable. Anecdotes from successful speakers reveal that stories can break down barriers and build connections in ways that data alone cannot.

Practical Applications

Collect personal stories and practice weaving them into your talks. Attend storytelling workshops and study the techniques of successful orators. Analyse your audience and choose stories that will speak to their experiences and interests.

8.1(d) Gestures and Body Language

The silent narrative of your body speaks volumes. Your posture, movements, and facial expressions can reinforce your words or betray your nerves. The more confident you feel inside, the better remains your outward demeanour.

Detail Expansion

Embrace purposeful movements, and let your hands accentuate your points. Stand tall, with confidence, and use space to your advantage. Align your nonverbal cues with your verbal message to create coherence and authenticity.

Evidence and Testimonials

Body language experts highlight the congruence between speech and physicality in renowned communicators such as Oprah Winfrey, Amitabh Bachchan and our very own Miss Universe Sushmita Sen. All of them use their entire being to engage with audiences, creating a powerful synergy between their words and the presence.

Practical Applications

Record your speeches and observe your body language. Seek feedback and refine your gestures to eliminate distractions. Practice in front of a mirror, and become comfortable with the physical aspect of your public speaking.

8.1(e) Audience Engagement Techniques

The energy of a room shifts when an audience is truly engaged. Your speech becomes a dialogue, a shared experience with those who have come to listen.

Detail Expansion

Ask rhetorical questions, invite responses, and make eye contact. Use humour wisely to build rapport. Tailor your content to the interests of your audience, making your speech relevant and compelling.

Evidence and Testimonials

Engagement can make the difference between a forgettable speech and a transformative one. Speakers like Tony Robbins excel in this area, often citing audience interaction as a key ingredient in their success.

Practical Applications

Incorporate polls, quizzes, or interactive elements into your presentations. Study your audience beforehand to understand their interests and tailor your speech accordingly. Practice active listening and responsiveness during Q&A sessions.

8.1(f) Handling Stage Fright

The rush of adrenaline before taking the stage is a natural response, but it need not be an insurmountable obstacle. History is replete with numerous examples and experiences of great speakers who began small and trepidations in their hearts.

Detail Expansion

Acknowledge your nerves as a sign of your investment in the outcome. Prepare thoroughly, visualize success, and employ relaxation techniques such as deep breathing or mindfulness. Rehearse until confidence replaces anxiety.

Evidence and Testimonials

Even seasoned speakers world over have admitted to experiencing stage fright. They often share stories of overcoming this fear through preparation and mental conditioning, turning nervous energy into a dynamic force.

Practical Applications

Join a public speaking group like Toastmasters and TALI to practice in a supportive environment. Develop a pre-speech routine that calms your nerves and centres your focus. Remember, a certain level of anxiety can enhance your performance, lending it a vibrant edge.

8.1(g) The Craft of Persuasive Speech

To persuade is to move people, to inspire them to action, or to adopt a new perspective. The aim is to convince the people listening to your point of view to perform in the manner expected.

Detail Expansion

Employ the classic rhetorical devices: ethos, pathos, and logos. Build credibility, connect emotionally, and present logical arguments. Structure your speech to lead the audience to your conclusion step by step.

Evidence and Testimonials

Historical figures such as Aristotle laid the foundations for persuasive speech, and these principles remain relevant even today. Effective persuasion, as practiced by leaders and activists worldwide, has the power to initiate change and influence society.

Practical Applications

Analyse famous speeches for their persuasive techniques. Practice crafting arguments for various viewpoints, even those you do not hold. Engage in debates to refine your persuasive skills in real-time situations.

Mastering public speaking is a journey, not a destination. Each exercise, each technique, and each moment of practice is a step towards becoming the speaker you aspire to be. Embrace the drills, immerse yourself in the process, and watch as the transformation unfolds. Your voice, your message, and your impact on the world await.

8.2 Applying Skills in Everyday Life

In the tapestry of our daily lives, communication threads through every interaction, binding us in a network of exchange and understanding. It's the foundation upon which relationships are built and maintained, careers are advanced, and personal fulfilment is achieved. With the art of public speaking as our scaffold, we venture into the realm of everyday life, applying its principles to enrich our every encounter.

Imagine weaving the finesse of a keynote speaker into the fabric of your daily dialogue. At the breakfast table, in the office, or during a casual chat with friends, you become a maestro of words, threading your ideas through the loom of conversation with grace and precision. This is the art of merging public speaking with daily interactions, a skill that can elevate your communication to new heights.

Public speaking techniques are not reserved for the stage alone. They are tools that, when used skillfully, can transform mundane exchanges into memorable connections. The clarity of diction, the resonance of voice, the power of storytelling, and the subtlety of body language are all instruments in your orator's toolkit, ready to enhance the way you communicate every day.

Consider Sarah, a software engineer, who often found herself overlooked in meetings. By adopting the posture and confidence of a seasoned speaker, she began to command attention; her ideas resonating with newfound authority. Or, as I remember my high school history teacher, who always incorporated storytelling into his history lessons. Suddenly, the past came alive for all the students, leading to increased engagement and retention.

Some may argue that the formality of public speaking has no place in casual conversation. However, it's not about grandiosity or verbosity; it's about the effective transfer of ideas. While one-on-one interactions may require a softer touch, the underlying techniques remain the same. It's about adapting these skills to fit the context and audience, whether it's a group of colleagues or a single child asking about their day.

Research supports the crossover of public speaking skills into everyday life. A study by the National Association of Colleges and Employers found that verbal communication skills are among the top attributes sought by employers. Moreover, the Harvard Business Review highlights storytelling as a critical business skill that can lead to more persuasive presentations and more effective marketing strategies.

Let's demystify some jargon. 'Diction' simply refers to the clarity and effectiveness of your word choice. 'Resonance' is about the fullness and richness of your voice. 'Nonverbal cues' are the silent messages sent through your body language. Understanding these terms empowers you to use them to your advantage in daily interactions.

To converse is to live; to communicate effectively is to thrive. By incorporating public speaking techniques into your everyday life, you can become a more influential thinker, a more persuasive leader, and a more empathetic friend. The clarity of your speech will ensure your ideas are heard, the resonance of your voice will command respect, and the stories you share will forge deeper connections. So, take these tools, sharpened on the stage, and apply them to the grand theatre of life. Your audience awaits.

As we journey through the pages of this book, we delve deeper into these techniques, exploring how to harness the power of public speaking to enhance our everyday interactions. Stay prepared, for the conversations you'll have tomorrow can be as impactful as any speech you might deliver under the spotlight.

8.3 Feedback Loops and Continuous Improvement

In the ever-evolving landscape of communication, the ability to captivate and persuade an audience is a coveted skill. Yet, even the most experienced orators know that the journey to excellence is never complete. Each presentation and each conversation is an opportunity to refine and perfect the art of public speaking. But how does one ensure continuous improvement in this craft? The answer lies in harnessing the power of feedback loops.

Imagine standing at the podium, your words flowing into the ears of an attentive audience. You've prepared, practiced, and performed, but the work doesn't end with the applause. The moments following your speech are ripe with potential—a chance to gather insights and propel your abilities forward.

The art of public speaking is akin to tending a garden. Without regular attention, the weeds of bad habits can choke the blossoms of eloquence and poise. Feedback acts as the gardener's shears, trimming away the excess and nurturing growth. Neglect this crucial step, and the garden of your oratory skills may wither, leaving you with a harvest of missed opportunities.

What, then, if the feedback loop is broken or non-existent? The consequences might not be immediately apparent, yet, over time, they accumulate. A speech might fall flat, a persuasive argument might fail to convince, or a vital connection with the audience might be lost. The cost of these missteps can be high—diminished credibility, weakened influence, and the erosion of confidence.

To avert such outcomes, one must actively seek and apply constructive criticism. The solution is a structured approach to feedback—soliciting opinions, reflecting on performance, and making iterative adjustments.

Begin by asking your audience to share their thoughts. What resonated? What could be clearer? Where did the engagement falter? Be open to what they say; their insights are the seeds from which improvement blooms.

Implementing this feedback requires a methodical process. Break down your speech into components—the opening, the body, the closing—and consider the critique for each section. Were your anecdotes compelling? Was your data persuasive? Did your conclusion inspire action? Armed with this knowledge, you can recalibrate, refining your message and delivery for the next occasion.

The efficacy of this approach is not a matter of conjecture but is supported by a wealth of anecdotal evidence and scholarly research. Take the inspiration from one of my mentees Mr Hiren, who started as a timid speaker but through the relentless pursuit of feedback, transformed into a conference headliner and a motivational speaker. His secret? He treated every piece of advice as a gift, meticulously integrating each lesson into his subsequent presentations.

Occasionally, one might encounter a situation where feedback is scarce or homogenous, leading to a plateau in development. In such cases, alternative solutions are necessary. One might record their speech, reviewing the footage with a critical eye. Peer review groups offer another avenue, providing a space for mutual growth among speakers. Technology, too, offers tools like speech analysis software that can measure pauses, vocal variety, and more.

As you embark on this journey of continuous improvement, remember the importance of variety in your sentence structures. Let questions punctuate your reflections: "How can I connect more deeply with my audience?" Allow vivid imagery to illustrate your points: "Visualize your words as a painter's brush, each stroke contributing to the masterpiece of your message." Embrace the rhythm and cadence of language, crafting sentences that dance to the beat of your intent.

Incorporating quotations can also lend authority and perspective to your narrative. As the renowned speaker Dale Carnegie once said, "There are always three speeches, for every one you actually gave. The one you practiced, the one you gave, and the one you wish you gave." Thus, let the feedback loop guide you from the speech you gave to the one you wish to give.

In summary, feedback loops are the lifeline of continuous improvement in public speaking. They allow us to see beyond our own perspectives, to identify blind spots, and to sharpen our skills. Embrace feedback with an open heart and a willing mind, for it is the compass that guides you to your destination—the pinnacle of oratory excellence. With each iteration, with each refinement, you come closer to the speaker you aspire to be—one who not only speaks but truly communicates.

8.4 The Role of Technology in Practice

The gentle hum of a smartphone app and the subtle red light of a recording device—these are the modern-day tools of the orator, as integral to the art of public speaking as the microphone once was to amplify the human voice. In a world where technology intertwines with every facet of our lives, it is no surprise that it has also made its mark on the realm of public speaking. It offers a plethora of opportunities to enhance one's skills, practice with precision, and receive instant unbiased feedback.

At the heart of this technological revolution is the proposition that with the right tools, anyone can refine their public speaking abilities more efficiently and effectively than ever before. This claim rests on the backs of countless apps, devices, and platforms designed to assist speakers in their quest for eloquence and impact.

The primary evidence supporting this claim comes from the multitude of apps that focus on various aspects of public speaking. Take, for instance, virtual reality (VR) applications that simulate audiences, allowing speakers to practice in lifelike scenarios without the logistics of assembling a real crowd. The palpable tension of a packed auditorium can be experienced within the quiet confines of one's study, complete with interactive audience reactions. Studies show that practicing in VR environments can significantly reduce public speaking anxiety and improve performance.

Delving deeper, these VR apps provide metrics and analysis on performance—vocal clarity, pacing, and even eye contact are recorded and evaluated. This immediate feedback offers a concrete basis for improvement, one that is often more detailed than a human listener could provide. This technological insight opens doors to mastering the subtleties of delivery that might otherwise go unnoticed.

However, there is counter-evidence to consider. Sceptics argue that technology may provide a crutch, creating a dependency that detracts from the authenticity of the speaker's presence. They warn of the loss of spontaneity and the human touch, elements that are essential to the art of oratory.

In response to these concerns, it is vital to clarify the role of technology—it is not a replacement for human feedback or the organic experience of public speaking, but rather a supplementary tool. It is there to be used in conjunction with traditional methods, to offer a different perspective, and to provide practice opportunities that were previously unavailable.

Furthermore, there is additional supporting evidence showcasing the benefits of recording devices—simple, accessible, and powerful. By recording their speeches, speakers can gain insights into their habits, both good and bad, and observe their performances from an audience's perspective. Playback can be a revelatory experience, revealing the nuances of body language, the power of pauses, and the impact of intonation.

Imagine the vivid imagery of a speaker's journey, much like an artist honing their craft—every recording, a brushstroke; every playback, a moment of reflection; every adjustment, a splash of colour transforming the canvas.

Do you ever wonder what your audience sees when you speak? How do your gestures translate across the room? How does your voice carry? By recording and critically analysing your performances, you answer these questions not through conjecture but through tangible evidence.

Admittedly, the overuse of adjectives and adverbs cannot capture the essence of a well-delivered speech. Instead, let the verbs carry the weight—'captivate,' 'inspire,' and 'transform.' These are the actions that technology helps you refine, with every practice session building towards the crescendo of your oratory prowess.

Even the rhythm and flow of your speech can be dissected and fine-tuned with technological assistance. The ebb and flow of your words, the delicate balance of pacing—these are the subtle elements that, when perfected, can elevate a speech from good to unforgettable.

Incorporating quotations from legendary orators can also serve as a reminder of the timeless nature of public speaking, even as technology reshapes its practice. Winston Churchill's famed "We shall fight on the beaches" speech is not only a testament to the power of words but also to the importance of delivery, a combination that technology strives to help speakers achieve. Yet again, I am reminded of the powerful motivational words of Dr Radhakrishnan on the Chinese aggression of 1962…. "We are fighting today, not for a piece of territory but for some fundamental principles………… .

In conclusion, the assertion that technology, including apps and recording devices, plays a pivotal role in enhancing public speaking skills is well-founded. Through the lens of credible evidence and verified information, it is clear that these tools offer invaluable support in the quest for oratorical mastery. They are not the enemy of authenticity but allies in the pursuit of excellence, providing new avenues for practice, feedback, and growth. With technology as a steadfast companion on this journey, the path to becoming a compelling, captivating speaker is more accessible than ever. Thus, we circle back to the central theme, standing firm in the belief that technology, when used wisely, is a powerful ally in the art of public speaking.

8.5 Joining Speaking Clubs and Groups

In the bustling city centre, where the sound of traffic melds with the chatter of pedestrians, there exists an oasis of eloquence—a speaking club known for transforming timid talkers into confident orators. Within these walls, professionals and students alike gather with a common purpose: to hone their public speaking skills and weave robust networks. Here, amidst the clink of coffee cups and the shuffling of chairs, experiential learning takes centre stage.

The central figures of this narrative are a diverse group of individuals, each bringing a unique story to the table. There's Joseph, a software engineer with brilliant ideas but a fear of public scrutiny; Radhika, a marketing strategist who seeks to refine her pitch; and Amir, a student whose dreams of advocacy are hindered by his quiet voice. Together, they embody the spirit of growth and the desire for change.

The challenge they face is universal—the anxiety of public speaking. For many, the mere thought of standing before an audience induces palpitations. Research shows that glossophobia, the fear of public speaking, affects a staggering 75% of the population. This fear can be a formidable barrier to professional growth and personal fulfilment.

The club's approach to overcoming this fear is multifaceted. Members engage in impromptu speaking exercises, prepared speeches, and constructive evaluations. Through role-plays and simulations, they confront and conquer their fears in a supportive environment. Each session is a step toward mastery, as feedback from peers provides the building blocks for improvement.

Over time, the results are noticeable. Joseph, once reticent, now articulates his ideas with clarity and confidence. Radhika's pitches have gained a persuasive edge, resonating deeply with her audience. Amir's voice, previously a whisper, now carries the weight of his convictions. Each story is a testament to the club's effectiveness, supported by the members' progression from anxious novices to adept speakers.

Reflecting on these transformations, it becomes clear that the power of such groups lies in their ability to mirror real-world scenarios while providing a safety net for experimentation. Criticism, when offered as constructive feedback, becomes a powerful tool for growth. However, one must acknowledge the potential for overdependence on structured environments, which can stifle spontaneity. The key is to strike a balance, using the club as a springboard to real-world engagements.

Visual aids, like recorded speeches or graphical feedback on vocal variety, serve to enhance understanding and offer concrete areas for improvement. These tools help members visualize their progress and pinpoint specific elements of their delivery that require attention.

The broader narrative that unfolds within the speaking club is one of personal transformation and collective empowerment. It echoes the age-old human desire to be heard and understood, to connect with others through the spoken word. The club is not merely a gathering of individuals seeking self-improvement; it is a microcosm of society, where voices are sharpened as tools for change.

As we close the chapter on this particular instance, a series of thoughts lingers: 'How might these newly polished skills ripple out into the world? Will Joseph's newfound confidence lead to innovation? Could Radhika's compelling pitches drive her company to new heights? Might Amir's advocacy inspire a movement'?

Joining speaking clubs and groups is more than a mere commitment to self-improvement; it's an investment in one's future, a stepping stone to becoming a mover and shaker in an ever-evolving world. The benefits are manifold—enhanced communication skills, expanded networks, and a deepened sense of community.

As you, dear reader, digest the essence of these shared experiences, consider your own journey. What holds you back from taking the stage? Can the camaraderie of like-minded individuals embolden you to find your voice? Perhaps it's time to step out of the shadows and into the spotlight, for it is there that you will truly shine.

Let this be your invitation to action, a gentle nudge toward the transformative power of joining speaking clubs and groups. Embrace the challenge, and watch as the art of oratory becomes not just a skill, but a gateway to a world of endless possibilities.

As Divya, a freelance consultant who has witnessed the transformational power of these collectives, I urge you to consider the ripple effect of your voice. The impact of your words can extend far beyond the confines of a club meeting; they can shape your destiny, influence others, and leave an indelible mark on the world. So, what are you waiting for? Join the journey of Public Speaking and let your voice be heard.

———⸨◦⸩———

CHAPTER 9

DELIVERING EFFECTIVE PRESENTATIONS

"The success of your presentation will be judged not by the knowledge you send but by what the listener receives.

—— Lilly Walters

9.1 Rules To Remember While Making PPT

Embarking on the journey to create a compelling PowerPoint presentation, you find yourself at the threshold of influence and persuasion. Your objective, clear as the dawn of a new day, is to craft a set of slides that not only conveys your message but also captivates your audience, leaving an indelible mark upon their minds.

Before you dive into the digital sea of slide creation, you must gather your tools—much like a painter assembles brushes and palettes. You'll need a computer with PowerPoint installed, a deep understanding of your subject matter, and a keen sense of who your audience is. Additionally, ensure you have access to high-quality images, pertinent data, and any other resources that will bolster your presentation.

Picture, if you will, a mosaic of steps before you, each one a vital piece of the grand picture you're about to compose. This broad overview serves as a map, guiding you from conception to the polished final product.

Now, let us delve into the heart of creation, where each step is a brushstroke on your canvas. Commence with a title slide that sings with potential, followed by an introduction that sets the stage for the narrative to unfold. Each subsequent slide should be a chapter in your story, with clear headings, concise bullet points, and visuals that serve as windows into your message.

As you weave through the tapestry of your presentation, heed these pearls of wisdom. Let simplicity be your guiding star; a cluttered slide is a lost opportunity. Prioritize contrast in text and background to make your words legible as if they were etched in stone and remember the power of the 'Rule of Three,' for it is in this number that concepts resonate and get retained in memory.

But what of the pitfalls, the snares that may catch your feet? Beware the lure of excessive animation, for it can distract more than it enchants. Keep your transitions smooth and your animations purposeful; let them serve your narrative, not dominate it.

How will you know if your masterpiece has achieved its purpose? Present it to a trusted confidant, watch their eyes, and listen to their feedback. The true test is in the understanding and engagement of your audience.

Should you encounter issues along the way, fear not. Common troubles, such as disproportionate images or inconsistent formatting, are but small stones on your path, easily removed with a little attention to detail and consistency.

As you step back, you might ponder, "Have I crafted a presentation that speaks of clarity and purpose?" Let the answer manifest in the reactions of your audience, in the questions they ask, and in the discussions that follow. A truly successful PowerPoint presentation is not just a collection of slides, but a bridge to understanding and inspiration.

Is your message as clear as a bell, and does your design reflect the essence of your narrative? Have you sculpted your words and images into a symphony that will relay through the minds of your listeners long after the curtains close?

Let the art of your presentation be a mirror of your dedication, a testament to the message that you hold dear. And when you finally stand before your expectant audience, know that you have crafted not just a presentation, but a journey through which you will lead them, slide by slide, into the dawn of understanding.

⬤

9.2 Overcoming Anxiety and Nervousness

In the quiet caverns of the human mind, anxiety and nervousness reside like unwelcome squatters, often invisible to the outside world yet powerfully influencing their host's every move. These emotional responses, while sharing similar physiological manifestations—a pounding heart, rapid breathing, and a mind racing with what-ifs—have nuances and distinctions that shape the human experience in profound ways.

Why compare anxiety and nervousness? To many, they may appear as two shades of the same colour, yet understanding their intricacies can lead to more effective coping strategies and heightened self-awareness. By dissecting their similarities and differences, one can navigate the complex landscape of emotional health with greater precision.

The benchmarks for our comparison will be their definitions, triggers, duration, and impacts on daily functioning. Through these lenses, we shall explore the common ground and the divergent paths these emotional states take.

At first glance, anxiety and nervousness seem to be twins. Both can be sparked by anticipation, whether of a forthcoming job interview or a performance on stage. They each can cause sweaty palms and an unsettling sense of dread. This shared ground reveals a fundamental truth: they are natural responses to perceived threats, hardwired into our survival instincts.

Yet, when we dig deeper into their character, the contrasts become evident. Anxiety is often a chronic condition that can seep into every crevice of one's life, sometimes without a specific trigger. Nervousness, on the other hand, tends to be a fleeting visitor, arriving in the face of an immediate challenge and departing soon after.

Imagine a painting, where anxiety is the background—constant and pervasive—while nervousness is a bold stroke of colour that demands attention but remains confined to a specific area. This visual metaphor helps us delineate their influence on our mental horizon.

What do these distinctions reveal? Anxiety, with its pervasive nature, can be debilitating, affecting one's ability to function. It may require a more structured approach to management, such as cognitive-behavioural therapy or medication. Nervousness, while uncomfortable, is often a temporary state that can be managed with deep breathing or positive self-talk.

Have you ever stood at a crossroads, heart pounding, as you contemplated the unknown? That sensation is not unlike the nervousness one feels before making a significant decision. Anxiety, however, is akin to a constant, low hum of apprehension, colouring every choice with a tinge of fear.

Their relevance in today's fast-paced world cannot be overstated. In an era where change is the only constant, anxiety and nervousness are frequent companions to many. Recognizing the signs and knowing how to address them can transform these emotional responses from obstacles to stepping stones.

To paint with words, let us consider the experience of Roshini, a young professional who often grapples with both states. She describes anxiety as "a fog that rolls in without warning, obscuring my clarity and leaving me feeling lost." Nervousness, she says, "is like the sharp bite of a winter wind—intense and bracing, but gone once I step indoors."

Why does this matter, you might ask? Because Roshni's story is not unique. Countless individuals navigate these emotional landscapes daily, and in understanding the terrain, we can better equip ourselves to journey through it.

In the orchestra of life, anxiety and nervousness are not always the lead instruments, but when they are, their presence is unmistakable. They can either cripple the melody or when acknowledged and addressed, add depth to the composition.

In conclusion, while anxiety and nervousness share a familial bond, they dance to different rhythms. By honouring their distinctions and learning their steps, we can move through life with greater ease and grace. The journey to overcoming these emotional challenges is not a sprint; it is a marathon that demands patience, understanding, and a willingness to continually learn from the paths we tread.

9.3 Handling Differences of Opinions With Public Speaking

In the kaleidoscope of human interaction, the art of handling differences of opinion with public speaking is akin to navigating a river with multiple tributaries—each choice leads to a distinct outcome, yet all are part of the same waterway. The ability to articulate thoughts and influence the minds of others is not just a skill but a tapestry woven with threads of empathy, strategy, and courage.

Imagine stepping onto a stage, the spotlight casting a warm glow on your face as a sea of faces fixates on you. The topic at hand is contentious, opinions are varied, and the air crackles with the tension of unspoken thoughts. How do you, as the speaker, bridge the chasm of contrasting views? How do you ensure that your message not only resonates but also fosters a spirit of understanding and mutual respect?

Firstly, consider the power of a well-crafted narrative. Stories have the unique ability to transport listeners to new realms, to allow them to experience perspectives beyond their own. As you weave your tale, let the vivid imagery of your words paint a picture so compelling that it draws listeners into a shared journey. "let us consider the example of a water channel splitting up a town and the two sides distrustfully looking at each other. But it was the bridge, crafted by the hands of those who dared to dream of unity, that brought them together." In this simple story lies a metaphor for bridging differences—a universal theme that finds favours with many.

Do not shy away from posing direct questions to the audience. "Whether they have ever been misunderstood because of their convictions?" These doubts lead us to a hint of commonality among the audiences. It is in these moments that barriers begin to dissolve.

When presenting your arguments, be mindful to limit the use of adverbs and adjectives that may carry unintended bias or diminish the strength of your claims. Instead, anchor your speech with robust nouns and verbs that stand unadorned yet impactful. "Because achieving the specific goal of public speaking is not to alienate minds but create a meaningful dialogue and consensus without hurting the different mindsets."

In emphasizing a key point, do not fear to employ a one-line paragraph. Unity. Let this word hang in the air, a beacon that draws your audience's collective gaze to the heart of your message.

Simplicity in language ensures that your message is accessible to all—eschew jargon and convoluted phrases. Remember, the river of understanding flows most freely without the obstruction of complexity.

The rhythm and cadence of your speech can underscore your message. A staccato of facts may highlight urgency, while a more languid pace allows time for reflection for a variety of ideas to merge and create new horizons of wisdom and conviction coming together.

Incorporating quotations or dialogues can add a layer of authenticity and depth to your presentation. You might quote the words of a renowned peacemaker: "We must learn to live together as brothers or perish together as fools," Martin Luther King Jr. once declared. Such words remind us that the endeavour to understand one another is both timeless and universal.

Show your audience the outcome of embracing diverse opinions rather than simply telling them. Describe the flourishing of ideas in a community that values varied perspectives, recount the tale of a dispute resolved through empathetic dialogue, or paint the scene of an innovative solution born from the marriage of seemingly opposing views.

Navigating the river of public discourse on contentious issues is no simple feat. It requires the skill of a seasoned captain who knows when to steer gently with the current and when to row against the tide. As you conclude your oration, leave your audience not with a sense of division but with the hope of convergence. "Let us build more bridges," you might say, "for it is on these that we walk together towards a horizon of shared understanding."

In the silence that follows, as your words settle like leaves upon the surface of a still pond, know that you have not just spoken but have also sown the seeds of change. The art of handling differences of opinion with public speaking is, after all, the art of transforming a multitude of voices into a chorus that sings the same song—a melody of mutual respect and collective progress.

9.4 Excelling Speech In Virtual Environments

Navigating the intricate digital landscape requires a compass of clarity and a map of understanding, especially when the terrain is the realm of virtual communication. With the ascent of technology, the pulpit from which we address the world is no longer made of wood and nails but of pixels and data packets. Here in this virtual environment, words are our emissaries and their meanings, our treaties of understanding.

As we delve into this uncharted domain, it's imperative to grasp the significance of key terminologies—words that serve as the bedrock of our discourse. Unpacking their essence will not only empower our dialogue but also ensure that our message traverses the digital divide with precision and resonance.

Virtual environments can sometimes feel impersonal. To combat this, speakers should actively engage their audience. Encourage questions, facilitate discussions, and use interactive features within virtual platforms that can create a sense of participation and involvement. In the absence of physical presence, your tone and inflection become powerful tools for conveying emotion and emphasis. A monotone voice can quickly lead to disengagement, so be mindful of infusing dynamism into your virtual communication. An engaged audience is more likely to retain information and find more value in the speech.

One of the fundamental aspects of effective virtual speech is maintaining clarity. Speak at a moderate pace, allowing your audience to follow your thoughts without feeling rushed. Pronounce words clearly and use pauses strategically to emphasize key points. To enhance clarity, speakers should articulate their words thoughtfully, avoid unnecessary jargon, and strive for concise expressions. This ensures that the audience can easily follow the message without the aid of non-verbal cues.

Incorporating well-designed slides, graphics, or multimedia elements can capture and maintain audience attention. Visual aids not only complement the spoken content but also cater to diverse learning preferences, making the message more accessible and memorable.

Effective speech in virtual environments is a multifaceted skill that involves mastering clarity, utilizing technology, engaging the audience, adapting to virtual dynamics, and emphasizing non-verbal elements. By incorporating these strategies, individuals can not only navigate the challenges of virtual communication but also excel in conveying their messages with impact and authenticity. In an increasingly digital world, the ability to articulate ideas effectively in virtual spaces is a valuable skill that opens doors to enhanced professional and personal connections.

9.5 Crafting A Great Elevator Pitch For Sales Professionals

Have you ever found yourself standing next to a potential client or investor, heart pounding, as the elevator doors close, and realized you had a fleeting minute to make an unforgettable impression? What if I told you there's a way to captivate their attention, make a lasting impact, and leave them wanting more—all before they reach their floor?

The art of the elevator pitch is often overlooked, yet it's a powerful tool in the arsenal of any sales professional. At its core, it's about weaving a narrative so compelling that your listener cannot help but be drawn in. It's not merely a summary of your product or service; it's an invitation into a story where your listener becomes the protagonist, facing a challenge only you can help them overcome.

Consider the sales landscape today: it's more competitive than ever, with countless voices clamouring for attention. Amidst this cacophony, how do you ensure that your message cuts through the noise? It's not about being the loudest; it's about being the clearest, the most resonant, and the most relevant.

Most people, when crafting their pitch, fall into the trap of listing features or spouting facts and figures. They believe that a comprehensive breakdown of their product's capabilities is what will seal the deal. However, this approach often leads to information overload, leaving the listener overwhelmed and disengaged.

Here's the real solution. The key to a great elevator pitch lies in simplicity and emotional connection. It's about finding the essence of what you offer and presenting it in a way that touches on your listener's needs and desires. It's not just what your product or service does; it's about how it makes their life better, easier, or more fulfilling.

As sales professionals, our goal is not merely to sell; it's to create a relationship, a partnership. It's about understanding the person on the other end of the pitch—what drives them, what concerns them, and what they're passionate about. And it's in this understanding that we forge a real connection, a bond that transcends the transactional nature of business.

Imagine, then, an elevator pitch that doesn't just talk at the listener but talks to them. Picture yourself presenting a solution so aligned with their vision that it sparks their imagination and stirs their emotions. That's when you've truly engaged them, not just intellectually, but emotionally as well.

You might be wondering, "How do I distil everything I want to say into such a short timeframe?" well according to me storytelling is the key. Paint a picture with your words; let them see themselves as the hero in a story where your solution is the key to their success. And remember, this narrative doesn't need to be complex; in fact, the simpler, the better.

Use vivid imagery to create a mental picture that sticks with them long after the elevator ride. Engage them with direct questions that invite introspection and self-discovery. As an example, a cryptic question could be to ask them about increasing the productivity of their organization by 25% within the same work schedules of team. Such questions not only pique interest but also present a direct challenge to their current situation.

Incorporate dialogue or testimonials to add authenticity to your claims. "Just the other day, CEO from ABC limited informed me that their business has been really energised, we've never been more efficient and more in tune with our customers' needs.'" This provides social proof and makes your solution more relatable and credible.

And let's not forget the rhythm and cadence of your speech. A mix of short, impactful sentences will grab attention, while longer, more descriptive ones will provide the detail and depth needed to truly convey your message.

Use the occasional one-line paragraph for emphasis, like a hammer driving home the nail of your key point.

Keep your language simple, avoiding jargon and technical terms that might confuse or alienate your audience. The last thing you want is for your listener to feel out of their depth. Instead, aim for clarity and accessibility, ensuring that your message is understood by all.

In the end, the goal is to leave them with a lasting impression, a curiosity that compels them to seek you out for more information. It's not about closing the deal in those few seconds; it's about opening a door and creating an opportunity for a deeper conversation where the real selling begins.

As a freelance consultant with years of experience navigating the challenges of sales, I've seen first-hand the transformative power of a great elevator pitch. It's not just a sales technique; it's an art form, one that requires practice, refinement, and a touch of personal flair.

So the next time you step into an elevator, remember that those brief moments could be the start of something monumental. With the right words, the right tone, and the right connection, you have the power to turn a chance encounter into a thriving business relationship. That's the magic of crafting a great elevator pitch for sales professionals.

CHAPTER 10

CULMINATION – INFERENCES

"Public Speaking is a skill that can be studied, polished, perfected. Not only can you get good at it, you can get damn good at it and it makes a heck of a difference."

Tom Peters

10.1 Public Speaking Redefined

In an amphitheatre thronged with eager listeners, a lone figure takes the stage. The air is charged with anticipation, the audience's collective breath poised on the cusp of release. This is the quintessence of public speaking, an ancient art that has evolved from the oratory of the Greeks to the TED Talks of the digital age. But what if we've only glimpsed the surface of what public speaking can be?

Our main assertion is this: public speaking has transcended its traditional boundaries. No longer confined to mere presentation of facts or persuasion, it has become a transformative experience that can reshape minds and inspire action in ways previously unimagined.

To support this claim, let us first turn to the evidence of history. In ancient times, orators like Cicero captivated the public with their eloquence, their words etching themselves into the fabric of society. Yet further let's remember the iconic speech of Swami Vivekanand in the 19th century in Chicago sensitising the world to religious tolerance and shunning fanaticism. Fast forward to the 20th century, and we witness Martin Luther King Jr.'s "I Have a Dream" speech, where the power of spoken words became a rallying cry for civil rights, echoing through the ages.

Yet, to delve deeper into this evidence, we must analyse the effects. Martin Luther King's speech did not merely present an argument; it wove a narrative that allowed listeners to envision a world of equality. The emotional resonance of his words galvanized a movement, proving that public speaking could wield the power to alter the course of history.

However, some might argue that these examples are exceptions, not the rule. Critics may present counter-evidence, suggesting that public speaking often fails to achieve such a monumental impact. Indeed, many speeches go unheard, and many words dissipate into the ether, forgotten.

In rebuttal, one must acknowledge these realities but also clarify that the potential for impact lies not in the frequency of transcendental speeches, but in the possibility of them. Each public address carries within it the seeds of change, whether they bloom into action is a matter of circumstance, delivery, and the readiness of society to listen.

Further supporting our claim, contemporary research in communication underscores the importance of storytelling and emotional connection in public speaking. A study by the Harvard Business Review highlights that presentations which utilise stories are 22 times more memorable than those that don't. This additional evidence suggests that the redefinition of public speaking is not just theoretical but practical and measurable too.

Drawing our exploration to a close, we reinforce our assertion: public speaking has indeed been redefined. It is a tool for change, an instrument for inspiration, and a vehicle for stories that have the power to move humanity forward. As we continue to bear witness to its evolution, may we embrace the responsibility that comes with it—to speak not just to inform, but to transform.

10.2 Achievers Are First Believers

In the chasm that lies between dreaming and achieving, there exists a bridge seldom seen but often crossed by those who dare to believe. It is not wrought of steel or stone but of something far more resilient: conviction. How often do we hear tales of individuals who, against insurmountable odds, rise to heights of success that stun the onlookers and even themselves? What is the thread that weaves through the fabric of such extraordinary stories? It is the undeniable truth that ACHIEVERS are, first and foremost, BELIEVERS.

Have you ever paused to wonder what powers the engines of those who accomplish the unthinkable? Is it talent? Perhaps. Is it the opportunity? Could be, or is it something more, something that resides within the core of their being? Yes, it is their belief—the unwavering faith in their vision and in their ability to turn that vision into reality. But do not be mistaken; this belief is not a mere wish whispered into the night sky. It is a loud declaration, a battle cry against the doubt that creeps into the corners of our minds.

Consider the story of Amelia, a girl from a small town with dreams as vast as the ocean. She gazed upon the stars, not simply with awe but with a yearning to dance among them. Her dream? To become an astronaut. Ridicule and scepticism were her constant companions, yet she held fast to her belief. "Why dream of the skies when you live on earth?" they'd mock. Amelia's response, a gentle yet defiant smile, spoke volumes. Why? Because someone must, and why not her?

Her journey was fraught with challenges, each one an opportunity to fortify her belief. Every failed exam, a lesson; every rejection, a chance to refine her resolve. And in those moments when the light of her dream seemed to dim, she found strength in a simple yet powerful mantra: " Failures Are The Stepping Stones To Success."

Similarly, is the awe-inspiring saga of the first Indian-born woman astronaut, Kalpana Chawala who hailing from a humble rural background aspired to break all social barriers and reached the pinnacle of the prestigious space shuttle Columbia not once but twice. Such is the tremendous power of indomitable conviction that glorifies the adage "ACHIEVERS are first BELIEVERS".

Why is it that this belief is so crucial, you might ask? It's because belief is the wellspring of action. Without it, dreams remain dormant, potential untapped, but with it, the impossible becomes an achievable target, one that is met with the arrows of relentless effort and perseverance. Amelia's and Kalpana's beliefs propelled them to study harder, train longer and reach further until one day, they found themselves donning a suit not of fabric, but of triumph, as they stepped into the spacecraft destined for the cosmos.

And what of you, dear reader? Have you nestled your dreams into the cradle of belief, or have they been left to wither in the garden of doubt? Let me pose a question that may stir the embers of a dream long dormant: What would you attempt if you knew you could not fail? Ponder this, for within its answer lies the kindling for your belief.

Belief is not a passive state. It is active, an ever-present force that demands nourishment. How does one feed this belief? Through the pursuit of knowledge, the acquisition of skills, and the seeking of experiences that align with your vision. It is a cyclical process; belief fuels action, and action, in turn, strengthens belief.

Yet, let us not be deceived into thinking that belief is infallible. It will be tested, shaken, and sometimes, it may even flicker. But it is in those moments, those critical junctures, that the true depth of one's belief is revealed. Will you allow the gusts of failure to extinguish your flame, or will you shield it, nourish it, until it burns brighter than before?

As we traverse this path of turning belief into achievement, let us remember the role of community. Surround yourself with those who fan the flames of your belief, who see the invisible bridge and encourage you to cross it. Distance yourself from the cynics, for their words are like torrents of water upon your fire. Seek out mentors, join hands with peers who share your vision, and create a collective belief so robust that it can weather any storm.

In closing, remember that the journey of an achiever is not a sprint; it is a marathon—a relentless pursuit that demands endurance, patience, and an unshakeable faith. It is a path littered with obstacles, but for those who believe, truly believe, it is a path that leads to the summits of success.

So, as you turn the page and continue your journey, ask yourself: Do I believe? And if you find that your belief wavers, look to the achievers who have come before you. Let their stories be the wind beneath your wings, for the first step toward achieving is believing that it is possible. Achievers are first Believers, and now, it is your turn to believe.

10.3 Follow The ABC Rule: Accuracy, Brevity, Clarity

Embarked upon the journey of transforming belief into achievement, one must hold fast to a guiding principle that serves as a beacon through the fog of complexity and confusion. This principle, the ABC Rule—Accuracy, Brevity, Clarity—is a triad of virtues that, when embraced, pave the way for effective communication and execution of any endeavour. As you venture deeper into this text, you will acquire the skillset to master these elements, thus propelling your aspirations from the realm of thought into the tangible world of results.

Let us first establish the goal that lies at the end of this path: to hone your ability to communicate and operate with precision, succinctness, and transparency. Whether you are drafting a report, delivering a presentation, or embarking on a new project, the ABC Rule will elevate your capacity to convey messages and execute tasks with utmost efficacy.

Before we proceed, gather the necessary materials or prerequisites: a notebook for jotting down key points, a highlighter for marking significant insights, and an open mind, eager to absorb and implement the wisdom contained within these pages.

Begin with a broad overview: the ABC Rule encapsulates three core elements. Accuracy ensures that your information is correct and reliable. Brevity compels you to be concise, avoiding superfluous details. Clarity demands that your message is understandable and free from ambiguity.

Now, let us dive into detailed steps, each dedicated to one of the ABCs, unravelling their intricacies and providing you with practical methods to integrate these principles into your daily practices.

Accuracy is the cornerstone of trust. It requires meticulous attention to detail and a commitment to truth. To master accuracy, one must:

1. Research thoroughly, using reputable sources to gather information.
2. Verify facts before dissemination, double-checking data and figures.
3. Credit sources appropriately to maintain integrity and authenticity.

As you tread this path, remember that accuracy is not merely about avoiding errors; it is about building a reputation of reliability that others can depend on.

Brevity, often mistaken for mere terseness, is an art. It involves expressing oneself with the fewest words necessary, without sacrificing the message's essence. To achieve brevity, one must:

1. Plan before speaking or writing, outlining the main points to stay on track.
2. Use active voice, which tends to be more direct and vigorous.
3. Eliminate redundant phrases and filler words that add no value.

In your pursuit of brevity, consider the wise words of French philosopher Blaise Pascal, who once apologized for writing a long letter, as he didn't have time to write a short one. True brevity takes effort and intention.

Clarity is the lens through which your thoughts are understood. It involves structuring your communication in a way that is easily grasped by your audience. To cultivate clarity, one must:

1. Know the audience and tailor the message to their level of understanding.
2. Organize thoughts logically, using headings and bullet points for readability.
3. Choose simple words over complex ones and define terms when necessary.

Imagine clarity as the light that guides your reader or listener through the forest of your thoughts. With each carefully chosen word, you illuminate the path ahead.

Offer tips and warnings: Accuracy requires a critical eye; do not accept information at face value. Brevity can lead to oversimplification; ensure that vital details are not lost. Clarity can be clouded by jargon; always opt for language that is accessible.

Testing or validation comes in the form of feedback. Share your work with a trusted colleague or mentor, asking specifically for insights on the ABCs. Their perspectives will serve as a mirror, reflecting the efficacy of your communication and the clarity of your thought processes.

In the event of troubleshooting, should you find your message misunderstood or your instructions not followed, revisit these principles. Is there a lapse in accuracy? Could brevity have stripped away too much context? Or perhaps clarity was sacrificed at the altar of complexity? Address these questions, and adjust accordingly.

As you wield the power of the ABC Rule, let your sentences dance with varying openers, paint vivid imagery with your words, and engage your listeners with direct questions. Opt for nouns and verbs that pack a punch, and employ one-line paragraphs for dramatic effect. Always aim for simplicity, crafting a rhythm in your writing and speech that is as natural as breathing. Where relevant, weave in quotations that lend authority, and dialogues that add life. Show the principles in action, rather than telling.

In conclusion, the ABC Rule is more than a mere guideline; it is a philosophy of communication that, when practiced diligently, becomes second nature. It empowers you to articulate visions, to share knowledge, and to lead with clarity. Now, as you integrate these principles into your life, remember: the road to achievement is paved with the bricks of accuracy, brevity, and clarity. Follow the ABC Rule, and watch as the doors to understanding and success swing wide open before you.

10.4 Build Your Personal Brand

In a world brimming with competition, standing out often feels like an insurmountable challenge. Yet, within the cacophony of voices and the myriad of faces, your personal brand is the lighthouse that can guide your audience through the turbulent seas of sameness. This beacon of individuality not only distinguishes you from the crowd but also establishes a trusted connection with your audience, whether they be customers, colleagues, or collaborators.

Before embarking on the journey of personal branding, consider this: the most resonant brands are built on authenticity and consistency. They harness the essence of an individual's character and project it outward in a way that is both genuine and compelling. To achieve this, one must be strategic. Herein lies a carefully curated list of key points that will serve as your compass in the voyage of personal branding.

1. Discover Your Unique Value Proposition
2. Craft Your Personal Brand Statement
3. Design a Visual Identity
4. Cultivate Your Online Presence
5. Engage with Your Community
6. Share Your Expertise
7. Monitor and Adapt Your Brand

a. The essence of your personal brand starts with understanding your unique value proposition (UVP). This is the foundation that distinguishes you from others in your field.

Your UVP is a clear statement that describes the benefit of your offer, how you solve your audience's needs, and what sets you apart from the competition. To unearth your UVP, reflect on your strengths, passions, and the aspects of your work that excite you the most.

Successful entrepreneurs and thought leaders often cite their UVP as the cornerstone of their personal brand. Take, for example, Steve Jobs' focus on simplicity and innovation, which became synonymous with the Apple brand.

Articulate your UVP in conversations, on your business card, and in all your marketing materials. It should resonate through every aspect of your public persona.

b. Your personal brand statement encapsulates your professional identity in a few succinct sentences. It's a promise of the value you bring to the table.

This statement should be memorable, punchy, and specific. It should convey your professional identity and aspirations, all while resonating on a personal level with your audience.

Effective personal brand statements are used by industry leaders to introduce themselves at networking events, in interviews, and when connecting with new clients.

Use your personal brand statement on your website, LinkedIn profile, and other social media bios. It's your elevator pitch to the world.

c. A coherent visual identity strengthens your brand and creates a lasting impression.

Consider the colours, fonts, and imagery that reflect your professional persona. Your visual identity should be consistent across all platforms and materials, from your website to your business cards.

Well-known personal brands, like Oprah Winfrey, have consistent visual elements that are instantly recognizable. They use the same colour schemes and logos across all platforms, enhancing brand recognition.

Apply your visual identity to your website, presentations, and any content you produce. It should be a visual echo of your brand's core values.

d. In the digital age, your online presence can be as significant as your real-world interactions.

Create content that reflects your expertise and UVP. Regularly be heard and seen on social media platforms to keep pace with your audience. Consistency and quality are keys to building a reputable online presence.

Professionals with a strong online presence, like Gary Vaynerchuk, leverage social media and content creation to amplify their brand and connect with their audience.

Regularly update your LinkedIn, Twitter, and professional blog. Share insights, comment on industry news, and participate in online discussions.

e. Interaction is a fundamental aspect of personal branding. It allows you not only to reach out to your messages but also to build a connection.

Engage with your audience by responding to comments, attending networking events, and participating in community projects. Show genuine interest in others.

Brands that excel in engagement, like Tony Robbins, create a sense of community around their brand, fostering loyalty and advocacy.

Be an active member of online forums in your field, attend industry meetups, and host webinars to connect with your audience.

f. Sharing your expertise is a powerful way to build your personal brand. Your authority in your field is established by the rapport that you build with your audience.

Write articles, give talks, and offer advice. By freely sharing your knowledge, you demonstrate your value and attract opportunities.

Experts like Brene Brown share their knowledge through TED talks and books, significantly enhancing their personal brands.

Guest post on reputable blogs, speak at conferences and run workshops. Each of these actions plants seeds for your brand to grow.

g. A personal brand is not static; it evolves with you and the market.

Regularly assess how your brand is perceived. Seek feedback and be willing to tweak your brand strategy to stay relevant and authentic.

Brands like Madonna's have remained relevant for decades by evolving with the times while staying true to their core. Such is the recent example of Priyanka Chopra.

Use social listening tools to gauge public perception of your brand. Conduct surveys or seek mentor feedback to understand how you can improve.

With each step you take toward building your personal brand, imagine you're creating a mosaic of your professional life. Each piece, whether it's your UVP, your visual identity, or the way you engage with your community, fits together to create a cohesive and compelling picture of who you are and what you stand for.

As you weave together the threads of your personal brand, remember to let the tapestry of your narrative unfold with a variety of sentence structures. Paint with words that conjure vivid images, craft sentences that spark curiosity with direct questions, and use strong nouns and verbs to create a lasting impact. Let the rhythm of your prose carry the reader through the journey, injecting life with authentic quotes and dialogues. Show the world not just who you are, but who you aspire to be, through the stories you share and the connections you make.

Your personal brand is a living entity, a story that you continuously write with each interaction, each decision, and each piece of content you share. It's a powerful tool that, when honed and wielded with care, can open doors to opportunities and pave pathways to success. Craft it with intention, nurture it with passion, and watch as it becomes not just a reflection of your professional life, but a beacon for your future.

10.5 Invest In Learning and Upskilling

In the heart of tinsel town, amidst the buzzing of early-stage startups and the shimmering facades of tech giants, there lay an inconspicuous building housing the ambitious venture known as "Vividha Skills LLP". The setting, a melting pot of innovation, was the ideal location for a company that aimed to bridge the gap between the soaring demand for high-tech skills and the workforce's ability to meet this demand.

The central figures of our narrative are the founders of Vividha: Swati, a seasoned tech executive with a keen eye for market trends and Anupam, a brilliant educator with a passion for learning methodologies. Together, they embarked on a mission to transform the way professionals approached personal development in a rapidly evolving job market.

The challenge was daunting. Technological advancements were rendering traditional education models obsolete and the workforce was struggling to keep pace. Employees found themselves trapped in a cycle of obsolescence and companies were grappling with a talent crunch.

Anupam and Swati's approach was revolutionary. They developed a platform that combined cutting-edge AI to personalize learning paths with a community-driven approach for peer support and networking. Their solution was not merely a set of online courses but an ecosystem that evolved with its users, offering mentorship, live projects and real-time skill tracking.

The results were impressive. Within a year, Vividha Skills had helped thousands of professionals to pivot to new roles or advance in their current ones and companies saw a marked improvement in innovation and productivity. Data showed a 45% increase in job retention and a tripling in the number of employees taking on higher responsibilities post Vividha Skills training.

Reflecting on these outcomes, it was apparent that the key to their success lay in its emphasis on adaptability and continuous learning. However, it was not without its criticisms. Some argued that the platform favoured those already tech-savvy and that it could widen the skills gap for those less familiar with digital learning.

To enhance understanding, Vividha Skills introduced visual aids. Infographics depicted learner progress and the skills most in-demand, while videos showcased success stories, lending a human touch to the data.

Connecting back to the larger narrative of lifelong learning, Vividha's case study served as a microcosm of the broader shift in professional development. In a world where change is the only constant, investment in learning and upskilling is not just beneficial but essential.

As we ponder on Vividha's journey, a question lingers: How can we ensure that the opportunity to learn and grow remains accessible to everyone, regardless of their starting point in the digital divide?

The sun dipped below the horizon, casting a golden glow over the Mumbai skyline. It was a reminder that every day's end brings the promise of a new dawn, much like the continuous cycle of learning. With each passing moment, the world changes and so must we, through relentless pursuit of knowledge and mastery of new skills.

In the grand tapestry of professional development, stories like that of Vividha Skills are becoming increasingly common. They serve as beacons of possibility, illuminating the path for those willing to take the leap and invest in themselves. They remind us that the future belongs to the perpetual learners, the curious, the adaptable and the bold.

As a leadership coach, I've seen firsthand the transformational power of upskilling. It's a journey of self-discovery as much as it is about acquiring new competencies. It's about building a mindset that embraces change rather than fearing it.

So, where do we go from here? How do we democratize access to learning and ensure that every professional, regardless of their field or experience level, can remain relevant and thrive in the face of technological advancement?

The answer may not be straightforward, but the pursuit of it is a journey worth taking. It is a journey that calls for collaboration, innovation and a steadfast commitment to breaking down barriers.

Let us then step forward with determination, for in the landscape of the future, the most valuable currency will not be money or status, but knowledge and the ability to adapt. And so, we must invest wisely in our most significant asset: ourselves.

And with that thought, I leave you to reflect: How will you invest in your learning and upskilling today?

EPILOGUE

As we reach the end of "Beyond The Pitch – Your Guide To Level Up Public Speaking Skills" it is time to reflect on the journey we have undertaken together. Throughout these pages, we have explored the intricacies of public speaking, dispelled myths, and equipped ourselves with the tools and knowledge to become effective communicators and leaders.

The journey of improving our public speaking skills does not end with the last page of this book. It is a lifelong pursuit, a continuous commitment to growth and self-improvement. The skills and strategies you have learned here are meant to serve as a foundation, a launching pad for your future endeavours.

Remember that practice is key. Every opportunity to speak in public, whether it be a meeting, a presentation, or a social gathering, is a chance to refine your skills and gain confidence. Embrace each opportunity with enthusiasm and use it as a stepping stone towards your goals.

Additionally, seek feedback and learn from others. Constructive criticism is invaluable in identifying areas for improvement and honing your speaking abilities. Surround yourself with mentors, coaches, and supportive individuals who can provide guidance and insights on your journey.

It is also important to adapt your skills to the evolving landscape of communication. With technological advancements and the rise of virtual platforms, the way we communicate is constantly changing. Embrace these changes and explore new avenues to showcase your speaking prowess. Embrace the challenge of connecting with an audience through screens and harness the power of virtual platforms to amplify your message.

Finally, remember that public speaking is not solely about the words we speak, but the impact we make on others for it is about inspiring change, leaving a lasting impression, and connecting with our audience. Cultivate empathy, understand the needs and desires of your listeners, and tailor your message to resonate with them on a deeper level. The power of communication not only distinguishes a social being from other living beings but also determines 'WHO WILL REACH WHERE, WHEN & HOW'!

As we conclude this book, I want to express my gratitude for joining me on this life-changing and metamorphic journey. I hope that the insights, strategies, and practical tips shared within these pages have provided you with the tools and inspiration to become a more confident and effective public speaker.

Remember, your voice has the power to shape minds, inspire hearts, and ignite change. Embrace the power within you, continue to learn and grow, and let your words create a ripple effect in the world.

Thank you for being a part of this transformative journey towards public speaking excellence.

AUTHOR'S BIOGRAPHY

Recipient of the 'CEO of the year' by MSME Business Excellence Awards 2023, Dr. Jaitly's string of entrepreneurial successes, make her a Youth Icon and a renowned Motivational Speaker in India. With 23+ years of experience across industries and multiple accolades, she is a personal brand to reckon with! Certified by Harvard and Wharton, she is currently a Board Advisor to many companies on Strategic Business Management and a qualified Independent Director.

A pioneer in bringing formalized Event Management education in the country, she is an Ex-Miss India finalist, celebrity interviewer and the only Indian woman who has presented Olympics twice for the National Television in India (Athens 2004 & Rio 2016)

Spearheading her own Corporate Communications firm focusing on Performance Consulting, Learning and Development for organizations worldwide, she is an Award Winning Pubic Speaking Coach, TEDx Speaker, Young Leaders Council Member at the All India Management Association (AIMA) and the former chairperson of the Indian Women Network at the Confederation of Indian Industry (CII) – Pune, Maharashtra.

With a background in business management and a deep-rooted passion for helping others succeed, Divya has dedicated her career to empowering individuals to become more confident, persuasive communicators and effective leaders. Driven by a belief in the transformative power of public speaking, she has made it her mission to dispel myths and empower individuals to embrace their unique voices.

As the author of BEYOND THE PITCH, she combines her expertise, personal experiences and research to provide readers with a comprehensive guide to becoming impactful communicators. Her writing style is approachable, engaging and relatable, making complex concepts accessible to readers of all backgrounds.

When she is not consulting or speaking, Divya can be found exploring the outdoors, immersing herself in nature and seeking inspiration from different cultures and perspectives. Her love for travel and exploration fuels her creativity and broadens her understanding of building human capital.

She positively affirms "Achievers Are First Believers"

Connect with her on

 Follow her on

 the_dee_show

 www.divyajaitly.com

RECOMMENDATIONS

Sunil Dutt, President | Reliance Jio Infocomm Limited

Divya is an amazing professional and a renowned Public Speaker. She combines knowledge at the conceptual level with applications and a great understanding of the industry across various categories of products and services. Divya brings professional expertise, empathy, and leadership to any task she gets on to and can manage multiple tasks at the same time. Have always enjoyed some very stimulating interactions during her motivational sessions. My best wishes are always with her.

Vijayaraghavan Sundararajan, Director | Process Automation & Process Mining | Barclays

Divya is my leadership & Public Speaking coach; she brings in astute insights to help me navigate the world of managing complex situations at work and personal front. Through her pressure-tested analytics and actionable insights, I have become a better version of myself. She is a great sounding board to bounce ideas and helped me glean through key events. I have been privileged and have benefitted immensely. Thank you, Divya, for your excellent coaching and insights.

Karthik Sathuragiri, Head of Marketing |AWS India

Divya has a tremendous presence as a public speaker and presents events extremely well. She leads with insights and provides direct feedback to her clients. She has a high degree of ownership and invests time and effort for prep and joint success. Look forward to continuing to engage with Divya!

Chitra Shringare, Global Head Utilities & Accounting Services | BNY Mellon

As a multi-talented personality, Divya is a true woman of substance. She is extremely skilled in devising communication strategies & learning solutions. She is a dynamic Public Speaker and a thought leader. My association with her is both professionally and personally motivating. Divya combines conceptual clarity with corporate solutions to enhance, empower, and energize growth potentials. Happy to be part of her journey.

David Buck, Chief Time Strategist | Infinity Lifestyle Design | USA

Dr. Divya is an expert in the science of effective human interactions. Using her public speaking and coaching expertise, she opens individuals and teams to realize their full potential in all forms of communication. Dr. Divya has a gift of bridging language and cultural gaps, creating greater understanding between people across the globe.

Rakesh Setia, President | Sales & Marketing | Rustomjee

Divya's work in the areas of communication, curating talk shows with industry leaders, and sharing through her sessions are commendable. Her session as a Motivational Speaker mesmerized the team. She established rapport with the entire team very quickly and shared some very strong real-life examples that made the team sit up and listen attentively. It was a fabulous session and the entire team not only enjoyed but also gained immensely from her perspective. In the end, the team really appreciated her ability to engage in real boardroom discussions and the fact that she came across as a serious business leader.

Anusha Acharya Madan, Strategic & Portfolio Lead for Global Talent, and Leadership Development | Siemens

Divya is one of the best out there if you are looking for a Leadership Coach or Public Speaking Specialist. I worked with her on a program for our future leaders to explore the power of stories and digital media to inspire and influence action. I found her highly experienced, passionate, and a fun trainer/coach. The coolest thing about her session was the fact that she was able to deliver some great tangible tips and actionable takeaways to build one's personal brand. I was impressed with how precise, sharp yet witty, and compelling her feedback to the participants on their personal elevator pitch was. Truly enjoyed our collaboration.

Narayan Govindram Jaesingh, Chief Business Officer | VSERV Digital Services

Had the pleasure of sharing insights & expertise with Dr. Divya on Leading & Managing Strategic Initiatives. Was inspired & awestruck by the quantum of research & knowledge exhibited by her as an integrated communication specialist & a public speaking coach. She always asks thought-provoking questions & will definitely be my 'Go to Person' on strategic consulting. Onwards & upwards!

Kedar Kulkarni, Business Analyst Chief Technology Officer | Barclays

I attended the Motivational Session by Dr.Divya & I feel blessed after attending her session on 'Mind full Vs mindful'. During the difficult Covid times, the entire experience was simply amazing. She really knows what she is presenting. It gave me a new perspective towards mindfulness. Kudos, Dr. Divya for changing & influencing my mind along with the team. Keep inspiring.

Shilpa Rao, Driving Access to Healthcare & Energy Transition |Serial Innovator| Purpose Alchemist

We meet many people every day, but only a few leave a mark, one of them is Dr. Divya Jaitly alongwith her cheerful positive personality. She can light up any conversation. I met her at the Strategic Initiatives masterclass where she was moderating our panel. She was well-researched, very articulate, and brought the best out of each of the panelists. Wishing her all the best in her future endeavors!

Dr. Charles Carvalho, General Manager | Human Resources | TATA Play

Divya is a high-energy Public Speaking coach who can connect with people with ease. She is well-read and manages to perfectly balance theory and application with ease. She will be an asset to any organization that wants to improve its communication capabilities. I wish her the best.

Minal Jagtiani, Founder of LeadThink, a solution that guarantees employability through a Talent-as-a-Service platform

At a recent online workshop on public speaking, which I attended, I was amazed at the intricateness of public speaking. And how it can create impact and influence amongst your audience. Dr Divya is the most patient guide and encouraging mentor. Her workshop was packed with learnings and easy-to-use tips, I recommend Dr. Divya to business managers and entrepreneurs who want to influence their teams, but most importantly, understand that self-growth for career and business is a personal responsibility.

Priyanka Gupta, Manager Projects at Siemens India | Leading | Mentoring | Customer Assurance & Credibility | CSR | Ardent Reader | Book Abstractor

Dr. Divya Jaitley is an exceptional coach for skills like effective storytelling, how to tone voice quality, how to deliver an impactful speech, and get your point across. She is an influential personality and coach with tons of genuine personal experiences. It was great associating with her for a day program and learning new things. I highly recommend her to people and organisations looking forward to coach themselves and their people to speak effectively.

Monica S, System Engineer | TCS

It was absolutely a great workshop on public speaking. I have learnt so many techniques to master public speaking skills from Dr. Divya.

Swastika Mukherjee, Head of Strategy, Sustainability & Marketing | Kennametal India

It has been a pleasure interacting with Dr Divya Jaitley. She is extremely professional, has the great ability to assess her coachee's strengths and available opportunities, and customize her modules accordingly. I have benefitted immensely from her sessions on leadership consulting and public speaking.

Surabhi Suman, HR Head/Director | IntraEdge India

Excellent training by Dr. Divya. Her attention to detail and minute observations with personalized attention and feedback are brilliant. Overall, the training sessions include all the aspects of public speaking to its best. Certainly, recommended for leaders, professionals, and students.

Ankit Singh, Business & Data Analyst |Stakeholder Management | ARA Security | Australia

I had a wonderful experience with Dr. Divya. The quality of mentorship is great here and one can't find better people for fine-tuning speaking skills. If you want your public speaking skills and overall personality to improve by leaps and bounds, Dr Divya is the ultimate choice as a Coach.

Vishwas Gundurao, Regional Sales Director – Teknion

I am currently getting coached under Dr.Divya on a public speaking online class. I am getting benefitted with her experience and some secrets of public speaking skills which everyone should know to gain confidence. In today's professional life public speaking is very much relevant and Dr.Divya is one of the best Mentor to get trained on it.

Mikhil Sarawagi, Founder & Managing Partner | Angel Investor | MJS & Co.

Dr. Divya is a very enthusiastic and dedicated professional. She kept us motivated us showed us the perfect path to go ahead in public speaking! Would always stay in touch and keep learning.

Pamela Ray Pawar, Professional Career Coach | Founder at The LearnEd Academy Professional

I attended Divya's motivational session during the Faculty Development Program funded by the Dept of Science and Technology. The topic taken up by Divya was so apt, as all knowledge is incomplete without good communication. Divya beautifully explained the concepts and was very insightful for me. I'm surely going to use these learnings in my work life for years to come. Thanks, Divya. Keep spreading your good work!

Dr. D.J. Edwin, Country Director at Help A Child

Divya is a dynamic speaker and thought leader, am glad to have associated with her, balanced with both management and people-centric. I like her humility too while she connects with all. Wishing you the best in all your ventures Dr. Divya.

Use Code **DJ407PS** To Avail Discount For Your Training
Sessions At TALI

The Advanced Learning Institute [TALI] is the brainchild of the credible
Leadership Expert, TEDx Speaker, Award Winning public Speaking Coach
& Former Chairperson at CII (IWN) Pune – Dr. Divya Jaitly. The institute
is a pioneer in performance consulting, offering end – to end solutions for
learning & development.

Our programs at TALI are future focused with a commitment towards
enhanced employee performance and bottom-line impact. We have worked
with more than 400 corporates and inspired more than 60,000 individuals
across the globe.

From corporate training to one – on – one mentoring sessions, team TALI
hand holds you through your personal and professional development journey.

Check out more at www.talinstitute.com

Connect with us to be a better version of yourself!

Introduction to the Public Speaking Self-Assessment Tool 

The public speaking classification system Sample Report is designated as follows:

BEGINNER: As a learner, you study the foundations of public speaking and diagnose reasons for why you lack confidence. You dive deeper into the three elements and start working on your communication skills to refine your pitch.

EMERGENT: You achieve an understanding of all the three aspects of public speaking, thereby refining your approach and mastering techniques to enhance your skills. You are able to deliver extempore speeches without any roadblocks.

INFLUENCER: At this level, you're satisfying both organizational and personal needs. That means as a public speaker, you are meeting the objectives for which you were hired, but you're also personally liked. You understand and are in control of all the three critical components of public speaking. The audience knows, likes, and trusts you.

PROFESSIONAL: Here you are a thought leader. You carry credibility and your reputation precedes you. Your hold on all the three critical components is par excellence and you are a respected expert with exemplary oratory skills. Very often you are invited at coveted events to present and speak on topics which are highly relevant.

Using the public speaking classification system above Sample Report, your report provides you with a look at the total of all the answers. Furthermore, the Public Speaking Self-Assessment also helps you see your strengths and opportunities in the visual, verbal, and vocal fundamentals (Figure 1). Each segment delivers a placement on the classification scale. After that, you'll have a summary of your strengths and options for consideration as focus items to help you be a more well-rounded public speaker (Figure 2).

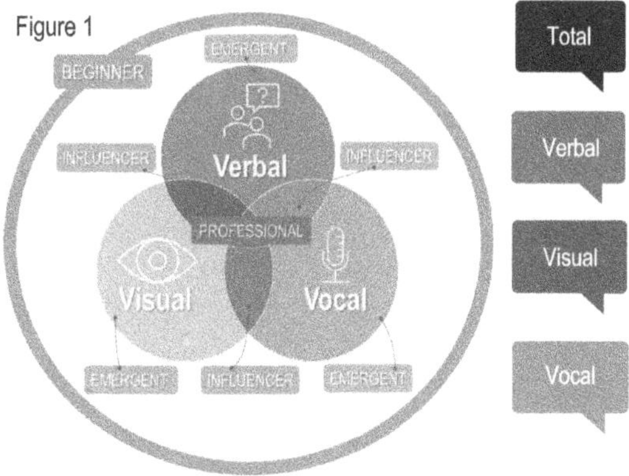

Figure 1

Figure 2

2022 Public Speaking Self Assessment, distributed by (TALI). Reproduction in any form, in whole or part is prohibited.
www.talinstitute.com

Take Your Assessment Today, email us at talktous@talinstitute.com

www.ingramcontent.com/pod-product-compliance
Lightning Source LLC
Chambersburg PA
CBHW040754120726
48005CB00012B/1166